Madhur Jaffrey's Indian Cookery

MADHUR JAFFREY'S INDIAN COOKERY

British Broadcasting Corporation

This book accompanies the BBC Television series
Indian Cookery, first broadcast on BBC2
from October 1982

Series producer and book editor: Jenny Rogers
Food adviser and food preparation: Moya Maynard
Illustrations: Fen Jackson
Photographs: Paul Williams

The BBC would like to thank the following
for the loan of equipment and accessories for the photographs:
The Covent Garden General Store, Long Acre, London WC2
Debenhams Limited, Oxford Street, London W1
Divertimenti, Marylebone Lane, London W1

Published to accompany a series of programmes
prepared in consultation with the
BBC Continuing Education Advisory Council

© Madhur Jaffrey 1982 First published 1982
Reprinted 1982 (twice), 1983 (three times), 1984 (three times)
Published by the British Broadcasting Corporation
35, Marylebone High Street, London, W1 M4AA

ISBN 0 563 16491 3 (paperback)
ISBN 0 563 16573 1 (hardback)

Typeset in Ehrhardt by Keyspools Ltd, Golborne, Lancs
Printed and bound in Great Britain by
Thomson Litho Ltd, East Kilbride, Scotland,
Colour origination by Excel Lithoplates, Slough, Berks.
Colour printed by Jolly and Barber Ltd, Rugby, Warwicks.

CONTENTS

CONVERSION TABLES

These are approximate conversions, which have either been rounded up or down. Never mix metric and imperial measures in one recipe.
All spoon measurements used throughout this book are level, unless specified otherwise.

Oven temperatures

Mark 1	275°F	140°C
2	300	150
3	325	170
4	350	180
5	375	190
6	400	200
7	425	220
8	450	230
9	475	240

Volume

2 fl oz		55 ml
3		75
5	($\frac{1}{4}$ pt)	150
10	($\frac{1}{2}$ pt)	275
15	($\frac{3}{4}$ pt)	425
20	(1 pt)	570
$1\frac{3}{4}$ pt		1 litre

Measurements

$\frac{1}{8}$ inch	3 mm
$\frac{1}{4}$	5 mm
$\frac{1}{2}$	1
$\frac{3}{4}$	2
1	2.5
$1\frac{1}{4}$	3
$1\frac{1}{2}$	4
$1\frac{3}{4}$	4.5
2	5
3	7.5
4	10
5	13
6	15
7	18
8	20
9	23
10	25.5
11	28
12	30

Weights

$\frac{1}{2}$ oz	10 g
1	25
$1\frac{1}{2}$	40
2	50
$2\frac{1}{2}$	60
3	75
4	110
$4\frac{1}{2}$	125
5	150
6	175
7	200
8	225
9	250
10	275
12	350
1 lb	450
$1\frac{1}{2}$ lb	700
2 lb	900
3 lb	1 kg 350 g

American measurements:

The British standard tablespoon (used in this book) holds 17.7ml, the American standard measuring spoon holds 14.2ml. Equivalent quantities are shown in the table opposite.

British	American
1 teaspoon	1
1 tablespoon	1
2	3
$3\frac{1}{2}$	4
4	5

The British standard $\frac{1}{2}$ pint (275ml) equals 10 fl oz (a British standard cup). The American and Canadian standard $\frac{1}{2}$ pint equals 8 fl oz (an American and Canadian standard cup). The British fl oz is 1.04 times the American fl oz.

INTRODUCTION

I have always loved to eat well. My mother once informed me that my passion dates back to the hour of my birth when my grandmother wrote the sacred syllable 'Om' ('I am') on my tongue with a finger dipped in fresh honey. I was apparently observed smacking my lips rather loudly.

Starting from that time, food – good food – just appeared miraculously from somewhere at the back of our house in Delhi. It would be preceded by the most tantalizing odours – steaming basmati rice, roasting cumin seeds, cinnamon sticks in hot oil – and the sounds of crockery and cutlery on the move. A bearer, turbaned, sashed, and barefooted would announce the meal and soon we would all be sitting around the dinner table, a family of six, engrossed in eating monsoon mushrooms cooked with coriander and turmeric, *rahu* fish that my brothers had just caught in the Jamuna River, and cubes of lamb smothered in a yoghurt sauce.

It was at this stage of innocence that I left India for London, to become a student at the Royal Academy of Dramatic Art. My 'digs' were in Brent and consisted of a pleasant room and through the kindness of my landlords, use of the kitchen.

'Use of the kitchen' was all very well, but exactly *how* was I going to use it? My visits to our kitchen in Delhi had been brief and intermittent. I could not cook. What was worse, I felt clumsy and ignorant.

An SOS to my mother brought in return a series of reassuring letters, all filled with recipes of my favourite foods. There they were, *Kheema matar* (Minced meat with peas), *Rogan josh* (Red lamb stew), *Phool gobi aur aloo ki bhaji* (Cauliflower with potatoes) . . .

Slowly, aided by the correspondence course with my encouraging mother, I did learn to cook, eventually getting cocky enough to invite large groups of friends over for meals of *Shahi korma* or *Shahjahani murghi* (Mughlai chicken with almonds and raisins). Once certain basic principles had been mastered, cooking Indian food had become perfectly accessible.

There is something so very satisfying about Indian cookery, more so when it is fresh and home-cooked. Perhaps it is that unique blending of herbs, spices, seasonings, as well as meat, pulses, vegetables, yoghurt dishes and relishes that my ancestors determined centuries ago would titillate our palates. At the same time it preserves our health and the proper chemical balance of our bodies. This combination of wholesome food and endless flavours and dishes makes Indian cookery one of the greatest in the world.

Indian food is far more varied than the menus of Indian restaurants suggest. One of my fondest memories of school in Delhi is of the lunches that we all brought from our homes, ensconced in multi-tiered tiffin-carriers. My stainless steel tiffin-carrier used to dangle from the handle of my bicycle as I rode at great speed to school every morning, my ribboned pigtails fluttering behind me. The smells emanating from it sustained me as I dodged exhaust-spewing buses and later, as I struggled with mind-numbing algebra. When the lunch bell finally set us free, my friends and I would assemble under a shady *neem* tree if it was summer or on a sunny verandah if it was winter. My mouth would begin to water even before we opened up our tiffin-carriers. It so happened that all my friends were of differing faiths and all came, originally, from different regions of the country. Even though we were all Indian, we had hardly any culinary traditions in common. Eating always filled us with a sense of adventure and discovery as we could not always anticipate what the others might bring.

My Punjabi friend was of the Sikh faith. She often brought large, round *parathas* made with wheat and *ghee* produced on her family farm. These *parathas* were sometimes stuffed with tart pomegranate seeds and sometimes with cauliflower. We ate them with a sweet-and-sour, homemade turnip pickle.

Another friend was a Muslim from Uttar Pradesh, known to bring beef cooked with spinach, all deliciously flavoured with chillies, cardamom and cloves. Many of us were Hindus and not supposed to eat beef. So we just pretended not to know what it was. Our fingers would work busily around the tender meat that covered the bones and our cheeks would hollow as we sucked up the spicy marrow from the marrow bones. But we never asked what we were eating. The food was far too good for that. On the other hand, whenever my father went boar-hunting and we cooked that meat at home, I never took it to school. I knew it would offend my Muslim friends.

Another member of our gang was a Jain from Gujerat. Jains are vegetarians, some of them so orthodox as to refrain from eating beetroots and tomatoes because their colour reminds them of blood, and root vegetables because in pulling them out of the earth some innocent insect might have to lose its life. This friend occasionally brought the most delicious pancakes – *pooras* – made out of legumes.

One of us came from Kashmir, India's northernmost state. As she thrilled us with tales about tobogganing – the rest of us had never seen snow – she would unpack morel mushrooms from Kashmiri forests, cooked with tomatoes and peas and flavoured with asafetida. She was a Hindu, of course. Only Kashmiri Hindus cook with asafetida. And they do not cook with garlic.

Kashmiri Muslims cook with garlic and frown upon asafetida. I found all this much easier to follow than algebra.

We had a South Indian friend too, a Syrian Christian from Kerala. She often brought *idlis*, slightly sour, steamed rice cakes that we ate with *sambar*, a pulse and fresh vegetable stew.

I, a Delhi Hindu, tried to dazzle my friends with quail and partridge which my father shot regularly and which our cook prepared with onions, ginger, cinnamon, black pepper, and yoghurt.

India is such a large country – over a million square miles of changing topography, divided into thirty-one states and territories. Geography and local produce have played a great part in forming regional culinary traditions. Religious groups within each state have modified these regional cuisines even further to suit their own restrictions. History too, has had its influences. Goa, for example, on India's west coast, was ruled by the Portuguese for four centuries. Many of its people were converted to Catholicism, some by Saint Francis Xavier himself, and eventually developed an eating style which included platters of Beef Roulade – a stuffed roll of beef cooked in garlic-flavoured olive oil. and a dessert of layered pancakes – *Bibingka* – made with egg yolks, coconut milk, and raw Indian sugar. British colonialists left quite a few dishes in their wake too. There were those *cutlis* (cutlets) that our cook made. He, of course, marinaded them in ginger and garlic first. Then, there was the strong influence of the Moghuls. They had come to India via Persia in the sixteenth century and introduced the sub-continent to delicate Pullaos and meats cooked with yoghurt and fried onions.

If there is a common denominator in all Indian foods, it is, perhaps, the imaginative use of spices. Does this mean that Indian food is always spicy? Well, in a sense it does. It always uses spices, sometimes just one spice to cook a potato dish and sometimes up to fifteen spices to make an elaborate meat dish. But it is not always hot. The 'heat' in Indian food comes from hot chillies. Chilli peppers were introduced to Asia in the sixteenth century by the Portuguese who had discovered them in the New World. Our own pungent spices until that time were the more moderate mustard seeds and black peppercorns. Those of you who do not like hot food should just leave out all the chillies – red, green, or cayenne – in my recipes. Your food will still be authentically Indian, superb in flavour and not at all hot.

The spices and seasonings that we *do* like to use in our food include cumin, coriander, turmeric, black pepper, mustard seeds, fennel seeds, cinnamon, cardamom, and cloves. Sometimes we leave the spices whole and fry them, sometimes we roast the spices and at other times we grind them and mix them with water or vinegar to make a paste. Each of these techniques draws out a completely different flavour from the same spice. This way we can give a great variety to, say, a vegetable like a potato, not only by methods such as boiling, baking and roasting but by cooking it with whole cumin one time, a combination of ground cumin and roasted fennel another time, and black pepper a third time. The permutations become endless as does the possibility of variety in tastes.

Does this mean that you cannot cook Indian food without having a whole lot of spices? I suggest that you start off with buying the specific spices you need to cook a selected dish and then slowly increase your spice 'wardrobe'. It is a bit like being a painter, I suppose. If you have a palette glowing with magenta and cobalt blue and sap green and vermilion, it will give you the confidence – and the choice – to do anything you want. You could use one colour, if you desired, or ten. It is the same with spices. It is nice to know that they are there. Whole spices last a long time. This way, you can cook aubergines with fennel seeds one day and green beans with cumin seeds the next day, if that is what you want.

Once you have mastered the use of Indian spices, you will find yourself not only cooking Indian meals but also inventing dishes with an Indian flavour and using Indian spices in unexpected ways. A French chef who once observed me cooking, now regularly uses ground roasted cumin seeds in his cream of tomato soup. I myself have created an Indian-style dish of pork chipolatas for this book to start you off in this pleasant direction. (See page 61.)

Since it is the carefully orchestrated use of spices, seasonings and flavourings that gives Indian food its unique character, it might be useful to examine them singly and remove their mystery.

SPICES, SEASONINGS AND FLAVOURINGS

Many of the spices used in Indian foods can be now found in supermarkets. These include cumin, coriander, turmeric, cloves, cinnamon, cardamom, nutmeg, black pepper, bay leaves, ginger, paprika, and cayenne pepper. Others have to be searched out from delicatessens and Greek, Indian or Pakistani grocers. Such grocers can now be found in all major cities and in many small towns as well. It is also possible to order spices by post.

Ideally speaking, it is best to buy all dry spices in their whole form. They will stay fresh for long periods if stored in cool, dry, dark places in tightly lidded jars. This way you can grind the spices as you need them. I use an electric coffee-grinder for this purpose although a pestle and mortar would do. The more freshly ground the spices, the better their flavour. If you can only buy ground spices, buy small quantities and store them, too, in cool, dry, dark places in tightly lidded jars.

When transferring spices from plastic packets to jars, be sure to label them. When buying spices from ethnic grocers, make sure that they are labelled. Many of my cooking students have come to me with unlabelled jars and asked, 'What do I have here?' Even I, who have been cooking now for twenty-five years, cannot tell the difference between ground cumin and ground coriander without tasting or smelling them first.

Here is a list of the spices, seasonings, and flavourings I have used in this book:

Asafetida
Heeng

The Indian source for this smelly resin has traditionally been Afghanistan and Western Kashmir. In its lump form, asafetida looks rather like the brown rosin my husband uses on the bow of his violin. Its smell is another matter. James Beard, America's foremost food writer, once compared the smell to that of fresh truffles. This seasoning is a digestive and is used in very small quantities. (It can even cure horses of indigestion!) A pinch of it is thrown into very hot oil and allowed to fry for a second before other foods are added. As asafetida can only be found at Indian and Pakistani grocers, I have made its use optional in my recipes. If you wish to purchase it, I suggest that you buy the smallest box available of *ground* asafetida. Make sure that the lid sits tightly on the box when you store it.

Cardamom, pods and seeds
Elaichi

Cardamom pods are whitish or green and have parchment like skins and lots of round, black, highly aromatic seeds inside. The whitish pods are more easily available in supermarkets. They have been bleached and have less flavour and aroma than the unbleached green ones. For my recipes, use whichever pods you can find easily, although the green ones are better. Many of my recipes call for whole pods. They are used as a flavouring in both savoury and sweet dishes. When used whole, cardamom pods are not meant to be eaten. We leave them on the side of the plate, along with any bones.

When a recipe calls for cardamom *seeds*, you can either take the seeds out of the pods (a somewhat tedious task, best done while watching television) or else you can buy the seeds from the few Indian and Pakistani grocers who sell them. If my recipe calls for a small amount of *ground* cardamom seed, just pulverise the seeds in a mortar.

Cayenne pepper
Pisi hui lal mirch

Made from dried red chillies, this is called red chilli powder by Indian and Pakistani grocers. Most of my recipes have a flexible amount of cayenne pepper in them. It is hard to know how hot people like their food. Use the smaller amount if you want your foods just mildly hot and the larger amount if you want it hotter. Cayenne pepper is sold in all supermarkets.

Chillies, fresh, hot, green
Hari mirch

These fresh chillies, 2–4 inches (5–10cm) long, green outside and filled with flat, round, white seeds, are sold by Asian grocers, some supermarkets and increasingly in street markets. Besides being rich in Vitamins A and C, they give Indian foods a very special flavour. If my recipe calls for them, make at least one good effort to find them. If you are unsuccessful, use a little more cayenne pepper as a substitute.

Green chillies should be stored unwashed and wrapped in newspaper, in a plastic container in the refrigerator. Any chillies that go bad should be thrown away as they affect the whole batch.

IMPORTANT: Be careful when handling cut green chillies. Refrain from touching your eyes or your mouth; wash your hands as soon as possible, otherwise you will 'burn' your skin with the irritant the chillies contain. If you want the green chilli flavour without most of the heat, remove the white seeds.

Chillies, whole, dried, hot, red
Sabut lal mirch

These chillies, about 1½–2 inches (4–5cm) long and ⅓–½ inch (approx 1cm) wide, are often thrown into hot oil for a few seconds until they puff up and their skin darkens. This fried skin adds its own very special flavour to a host of meats, vegetables, and pulses. Handle these chillies carefully, making sure that you wash your hands well before you touch your face. If you want the flavour of the chillies without their heat, make a small opening in them and then shake out and discard their seeds.

These chillies are sold by most Asian grocers and in many supermarkets.

Cinnamon
Dar cheeni

Buy sticks. We often use them whole in meat and rice dishes. The sticks are used just for their flavour and aroma and are not meant to be eaten. They can be found in all supermarkets.

Cloves, whole
Long

We often use whole cloves in our meat and rice dishes for their flavour and aroma. They are not meant to be eaten. (It must be added that we do suck on cloves as a mouth freshener.) Whole cloves are sold by most supermarkets.

Coconut, fresh grated
Nariyal

When buying coconuts, make sure that they are crack-free and have no mould on them. Shake them to make sure that they are heavy with liquid. Now hold a coconut in one hand over a sink and hit it around the centre with the claw end of a hammer or with the blunt side of a heavy cleaver. The coconut should crack and break into two halves. (You could, if you like, collect the liquid in a cup. It is not used in cooking, but you may drink it. I do. I consider it my reward for breaking open the coconut in the first place.) Taste a piece of the coconut to make sure it is sweet and not rancid. Prise off the coconut flesh from the hard shell with a knife. If it proves to be too obstinate, it helps to put the coconut halves, cut side up, directly over a low flame, turning them around now and then so they char slightly. The woody shell contracts and releases the kernel.

Now peel off the brown coconut skin with a potato peeler and break the flesh into 1 inch (2.5cm) pieces (larger ones if you are grating manually). Wash off these coconut pieces and either grate them finely on a hand grater or else put them in an electric blender or food processor. Do not worry about turning them into pulp in these electric machines. What you will end up with will be very finely 'grated' coconut, perfect for all the Indian dishes that require it.

Grated coconut freezes beautifully and defrosts fast. I always grate large quantities whenever I have the time and store it in the freezer for future use.

Fresh coconuts are sold by all Asian grocers and are widely available in ordinary greengrocers' shops.

Coriander, fresh green

Hara dhaniya or *Kothmir*

This is one of India's favourite herbs and is used, just as parsley might be, both as a garnish and for its flavour. This pretty green plant grows about 6–8 inches (15–20cm) in height. Just the top, leafy section is used, though the stems are sometimes thrown into pulse dishes for their aroma. This herb is worth hunting for as its delicate flavour is unique. It is sold by Asian grocers, but it may also be grown at home from coriander seeds.

To store fresh green coriander, put it in its unwashed state, roots and all, into a container filled with water, almost as if you were putting flowers in a vase. The leafy section of the plant should not be in water. Pull a polythene bag over the coriander and container and re-frigerate the whole thing. The fresh coriander should last for weeks. Every other day, pick off and discard the yellowing leaves. If you cannot find fresh coriander, use parsley as a substitute.

Coriander seeds, whole and ground

Dhania, sabut and pisa

These are the round, beige seeds of the coriander plant. They are used a lot in Indian cooking, generally in their ground form. You may buy them, already ground, from supermarkets and Indian and Pakistani grocers. You could also buy the whole seeds and grind them yourself in small quantities in an electric coffee-grinder. I like to put my home-ground coriander seeds through a sieve though this is not essential.

Ground coriander seeds, if stored for several months, begin to taste a little like sawdust. It is best to discard them at this stage and start off with a fresh batch.

Cumin seeds, whole and ground

Zeera, sabut and pisa

These caraway-like seeds are used very frequently in Indian food, both in their whole and ground forms. The whole seeds are sold by Indian and Pakistani grocers and by some supermarkets. The ground seeds can be found in nearly all supermarkets. Whole seeds keep their flavour much longer and may be ground very easily in an electric coffee-grinder.

Roasted cumin seeds

Put 4–5 tablespoons of whole cumin seeds into a small, heavy frying pan (cast-iron frying pans are best for this) and place the pan over a medium flame. No fat is necessary. Stir the seeds and keep roasting them until they turn a few shades darker. Soon you will be able to recognise the wonderful 'roasted' aroma that these seeds emit when they are ready. Store in an airtight container.

Ground roasted cumin seeds

Empty the roasted seeds into an electric coffee-grinder or other spice grinder and grind them finely. You could also use a pestle and mortar for this or else put the seeds between two sheets of brown paper and crush them with a rolling pin. Store ground roasted cumin seeds in a tightly lidded jar.

Cumin seeds, black
Shah zeera or *Kala zeera*

These fine seeds, darker and more expensive than regular cumin seeds, are sold only by Indian and Pakistani grocers. They look like caraway seeds but have a gentle flavour. Buy them whole. If you cannot find them, use regular cumin seeds as a substitute.

Fennel seeds
Sonf

These seeds taste and look like anise seeds only they are larger, plumper, and milder. They give meat and vegetables a delicious, liquorice like flavour. They may be bought from some supermarkets and all Indian and Pakistani grocers.

Indians often serve roasted fennel seeds at the end of a meal as a digestive and mouth freshener.

Garam masala

This is an aromatic mixture that generally incorporates spices which are supposed to heat the body (the words mean 'hot spices') such as large black cardamoms, cinnamon, black cumin (also called *shah zeera* or royal cumin), cloves, black peppercorns and nutmeg. The mixture is used sparingly and is generally put into foods towards the end of their cooking period. It is also used as a garnish – a final aromatic flavouring sprinkled over cooked meats, vegetables and pulses.

Garam masala is not a standardized spice mixture. Apart from the fact that there are many regional variations, I am sure that every North Indian and Pakistani home has its own family recipe. The recipe here happens to be one of my favourites. I have substituted seeds from the green cardamom pods for the more traditional black ones as I find their taste to be far more delicate.

Indian and Pakistani grocers and some supermarkets do sell a ready-made *garam masala* which you may certainly resort to in emergencies. However, you will find it quite pallid, as cheaper spices, such as cumin and coriander are often substituted for the more expensive cardamom and cloves.

It is best to grind *garam masala* in small quantities so that it stays fresh. My recipe makes about 3 tablespoons.

1 tablespoon cardamom seeds
A 2 inch (5cm) stick of cinnamon
1 teaspoon black cumin seeds (use regular cumin seeds as a substitute)
1 teaspoon whole cloves
1 teaspoon black peppercorns
$\frac{1}{4}$ of an average-sized nutmeg

Place all the ingredients in a clean, electric coffee-grinder (or any other spice grinder). Turn the machine on for 30–40 seconds or until the spices are finely ground. Store in a small jar with a tight-fitting lid. Keep away from heat and sunlight.

Ginger, dried ground
Sonth

This is ginger that is dried and powdered, the same that you might use to make ginger bread. It is available in all supermarkets.

Ginger, fresh
Adrak

This light brown, knobbly 'root' is not a root at all but a rhizome with a refreshing, pungent flavor. Its potato-like skin needs to be peeled away before it can be chopped, sliced, grated, or made into a paste. To grate ginger into a pulp, use the finest part of a hand grater. To grind ginger into a paste, chop it coarsely first and then throw it into the container of a food processor or blender. Add just enough water to make as smooth a paste as possible.

Fresh ginger, a very common ingredient in Indian cooking, is now sold by many super-markets. It is certainly sold by all Asian grocers. When buying ginger, look for pieces that are not too wrinkled but have a taut skin. If you use ginger infrequently, 'store' ginger by planting it in a somewhat dry, sandy soil. Water it infrequently. Your ginger will not only survive, but will also sprout fresh knobs. Whenever you need some, dig it up, break off a knob, and then plant the rest again. If you use ginger frequently, store it in a cool, airy basket, along with your onions, potatoes, and garlic.

Kalonji

This spice is a small, black, teardrop shaped onion seed with an appealing, earthy aroma. It is used for cooking vegetable and fish dishes in Bengal. The rest of the country uses it for pickling. Some north Indian breads such as *naans* have these seeds sprinkled on them before they are baked. *Kalonji* is sold in Indian and Pakistani stores.

Mustard oil
Sarson ka tel

This yellow oil made from mustard seeds is quite pungent when raw and amazingly sweet when heated to a slight haze. It is used in Bengal and Kashmir for cooking vegetables and fish. It is the favourite oil throughout India for pickling. It is available only at Indian and Pakistani grocers. If you cannot find it, ground-nut oil may be substituted.

Mustard seeds, whole black
Sarson

Once you start using these seeds, you will not want to stop. They are round, tiny, and not really black but a dark reddish-brown colour. When scattered into hot oil they turn deliciously nutty. If you want to know what they taste like in isolation, make the carrot salad on page 170. They are the main seasoning in that dish. Mustard seeds are available at Indian and Pakistani grocers.

Nutmeg
Jaiphal

Buy whole nutmegs. They are sold in many supermarkets, fine delicatessens, and all Indian and Pakistani stores. If a recipe calls for a third of a nutmeg, just hit a nutmeg lightly with a hammer. It is very soft and breaks quite easily.

Saffron
Zaafraan or *Kesar*

Saffron threads are the stigma of special crocuses that, in India, grow in the northern state of Kashmir. Saffron *is* expensive. It is used in festive dishes both for its saffron colour and its aroma. Yellow food colouring, or a small pinch of turmeric, may be substituted for the real thing even though purists would disapprove.

To get the most colour and flavour out of saffron, Indians often roast the threads lightly in a heavy cast-iron frying pan and then crumble them into a small amount of hot milk. This milk is then poured into rice and meat dishes as well as desserts.

Saffron is sold in some supermarkets, all fine delicatessens and most Indian and Pakistani groceries. Powdered saffron is also available in selected shops.

Salt

Amounts of salt given in recipes can be adjusted to suit individual tastes.

Sesame seeds
Til

I use the beige, unhulled seeds that are sold in all health food stores and all Oriental grocers. They have a wonderful, nutty flavour, specially after they have been roasted.

Turmeric
Haldi

This is the spice that makes many Indian foods yellow. Apart from its mild, earthy flavour, it is used mainly because it is a digestive and an antiseptic. Fresh turmeric looks like the baby sister of fresh ginger. They are both rhizomes. The only kind of turmeric I have seen in Britain is the dried variety. Buy the ground kind. Use it carefully as it can stain. It is sold in all supermarkets.

Vark

This airy, real silver tissue is used for garnishing sweets as well as festive meat and rice dishes. It is sold only at some Indian and Pakistani grocers. Each silver tissue is packed between sheets of paper. Remove the top sheet carefully. Then pick up the next sheet with the *vark* on it and overturn it gently on the food you wish to garnish. Try not to let the *vark* disintegrate. It *is* edible. Store it in a tightly closed tin as it can tarnish.

Vegetable oil

Most of my recipes call, rather generally, for vegetable oil. You could use what is labelled as vegetable oil in the supermarkets or you could use ground-nut oil, corn oil or sunflower oil. All would be quite suitable.

Yellow and red food colourings

These are used on some Indian foods – for instance these give Tandoori food its distinctive colouring. They are vegetable colourings and have no taste. However, one word of warning: a few people (and that includes me!) are allergic to the tartrazine contained in these colourings.

TECHNIQUES

Indian food is unique in its imaginative use of spices, seasonings, and flavourings. Many of our cooking techniques are really ways of getting these same spices, seasonings and flavourings to yield as great a variety of tastes and textures as possible. Spices and herbs do not have single, limited tastes. Depending upon how they are used – whole, ground, roasted, fried – they can be coaxed into producing a much larger spectrum than you might first imagine. Herein lies the genius of Indian cooking.

It amuses me to find that many of the techniques used in the 'Nouvelle Cuisine' of France have been used in India for centuries. We are told that sauces can be made much lighter if they are thickened with ingredients other than flour. Flour is almost never used as a thickener for Indian sauces. Instead, we have used, very cleverly, I might add, ingredients such as onions, garlic, ginger, yoghurt and tomatoes.

I think it might be useful, before you actually start cooking a recipe from this book, to measure and prepare all the ingredients you need for the recipe and have them ready near the cooker. Once you are experienced, this will not matter as much. But for those of you who are new to Indian cookery, it will help if you make all your pastes and do all your chopping and measuring before you start. The reason for this is that many Indian dishes require you to cook in one, flowing sweep. Ingredient follows ingredient, often swiftly. Frequently there is no time to stop and hunt for a spice that is hidden in the back of a cupboard. Something on the cooker might burn if you do. So organize yourself and read the recipe carefully. If many of the ingredients go into the pot at the same time, you can measure them out and keep them in the same bowl or plate.

Here are some of the more commonly used techniques:

Clarified butter
Ghee

Not all Indian food is cooked in *ghee*, as some people imagine. Many of our foods are *meant* to be cooked in vegetable oil. But *ghee* does have a rich, nutty taste and a spoonful of it is frequently put on top of cooked pulses to enrich them and give them a silky smoothness. I must add here that there are certain families in India (not ours) who have always cooked in *ghee*. There used to be a certain amount of status attached to being able to say, 'We use nothing but pure *ghee*.' But today, even these families are coming around to using unsaturated fats.

I feel that cooking in *ghee* is a bit like cooking in butter. It is fine to do it some of the time for certain selected dishes. Some of my recipes do call for *ghee*. I suggest you buy it, ready-made, from Asian grocers. However, if you wish to make it yourself, melt a pound of unsalted butter in a small, heavy pot over a low flame. Then let it simmer very gently for 10–30 minutes. The length of the time will depend upon the amount of water in the butter. As soon as the white, milky residue turns to golden particles (you have to keep watching), strain the *ghee* through several layers of cheesecloth or a large handkerchief. Cool and then pour into a clean jar. Cover. Properly made *ghee* does not need refrigeration.

Dropping spices into hot oil
Baghaar

I do not know of this technique being used anywhere else in the world. Oil (or *ghee*) is heated until it is extremely hot, but not burning. Then spices, generally whole ones, or else chopped up garlic and ginger, are added to the oil. The seasonings immediately begin to swell, brown, pop, or otherwise change character. This seasoned oil, together with all the spices in it, is then poured over cooked foods such as pulses and vegetables or else uncooked foods are added to it and then sautéed or simmered. The seasonings that are most commonly used for *baghaar* include whole cumin seeds, whole black mustard seeds, whole fennel seeds, whole dried red chillies, whole cloves, cinnamon sticks, cardamom pods, bay leaves, black peppercorns, as well as chopped up garlic and ginger. Hot oil transforms them all and gives them a new, more concentrated character. When the whole spices used are large, such as bay leaves, cinnamon sticks or even cloves and peppercorns, they are not meant to be eaten but are left to one side of the plate along with any bones.

Grinding spices

Many recipes call for ground spices. In India, we generally buy our spices whole and then grind them ourselves as we need them. They have much more flavour this way. You probably already know the difference between freshly ground black pepper and ground pepper that has been sitting around for a month. The same applies to all spices. In India, the grinding of spices is generally done on heavy grinding stones. We, in our modern kitchens, can get the same results without the labour by using an electric coffee-grinder. It is best to grind limited quantities so that the spices do not lose their flavour. If you wipe the grinder carefully after use there will be no 'aftertaste' of spices to flavour your coffee beans.

Buying ground spices is perfectly all right as long as you know that they will be less potent as time goes on. Before buying your spices, consult the preceding chapter to see which spices you must buy whole and which you may buy ground.

Roasting spices

This brings out yet another flavour from the spices. In my home, for example, we always make yoghurt relishes with cumin that has been roasted first and then ground. Nothing else will do. Ordinary ground cumin has a different flavour, quite unsuitable for putting into foods that are not going to be cooked. This roasting is best done in a heavy, cast iron frying pan since the pan can be heated without putting oil or water into it first. Whole spices are put into the pan. The pan is then shaken around until the spices turn a shade or two darker and emit their new 'roasted' aroma. You will begin to recognise it after you have done it a few times.

Making thick sauces

Many of our meat, poultry, and fish dishes have thick, dark sauces. My mother always said that the mark of a good chef was his sauce which depended not only on a correct balance of all the ingredients, but the correct frying (*bhuno*-ing) of these ingredients.

As I stated earlier, there is no flour in these sauces. The 'body' comes, very often, from onions, garlic and ginger. The rich brown colour comes from frying all these ingredients properly. Very often, we make a paste of one or more of these ingredients first. In India, this is done on a grinding stone but in western kitchens it can be done easily in food processors and blenders, sometimes with the aid of a little water.

Once the paste has been made, it needs to be browned or the sauce will not have the correct flavour and colour. This is best done in a heavy pot, preferably non-stick, in a *generous* amount of oil. Remember that extra oil can always be spooned off the top once the dish has been cooked.

Browning sliced or chopped onions and garlic

Sometimes a recipe requires that you brown thinly sliced or chopped onions. I have noticed that many of the students in my cookery classes stop half-way and when I point out to them that the onions are not quite done, they say 'Oh, but if we cook them more, they will burn.' They will not, not if you watch. Start the frying on a medium-high flame and turn the heat down somewhat as the onions lose their water and begin to turn brown. They do need to be a rich reddish-brown colour or your sauce – if that is what they are intended for – will be pale and weak.

The same goes for garlic. There is a common misconception that if garlic is allowed to pick up any colour at all, it will turn bitter. Actually, garlic tastes quite superb if it is chopped and allowed to fry in oil until it turns a medium-brown colour. I often cook courgettes this way – in oil that has been flavoured with browned garlic. Spinach and cauliflower tastes good this way too. In India, we say that such dishes are cooked with a garlic *baghaar*. A garlic *baghaar* can, of course, just be the first step in a recipe. More spices would be added later.

Adding yoghurt to sauces

Yoghurt adds a creamy texture and a delicate tartness to many of our sauces. But yoghurt curdles when it is heated. So when we add it to our browning sauces, we add just a tablespoon at a time. After a tablespoon of yoghurt has been put in, it is stirred and fried until it is absorbed and 'accepted' by the sauce. Then the next tablespoon is added.

Peeling and chopping tomatoes

Many of my recipes call for peeled and chopped tomatoes. To peel them, bring a pot of water to a rolling boil. Drop in the tomatoes for 15 seconds. Drain, rinse under cold water and peel. Now chop the tomatoes, making sure that you save all the juice that comes out of them. In India, we very rarely seed tomatoes. Many people do not even bother to peel them though I do feel that this improves the texture of a sauce.

Reducing sauces

Sometimes meat is allowed to cook in a fairly thin, brothy sauce. Then the lid of the pot is removed and the sauce reduced over a fairly high flame until it is thick and clings to the meat. The meat has to be stirred frequently at this stage, so that it does not catch and burn.

Cooking chicken without its skin

In India, we almost always remove the skin of the chicken before we cook it. The flavour of the spices penetrates the chicken much better this way and the entire dish is less fatty. It is very easy to remove the skin. Just hold it with kitchen paper so that it does not slip, and pull!

Marinading

We often cut deep gashes in large pieces of meat and leave them overnight in a marinade of yoghurt and seasonings. The yoghurt tenderises the meat while the gashes allow the flavour to penetrate deep inside the meat. After this, the meat can be grilled or baked faster than usual.

Browning meats

In India, we generally do not brown cubes of meat by themselves but brown them with the sauce instead. I find this hard to do with British meats because they release far too much water as they cook. Indian meats tend to be very fresh and have far less water in them. So to avoid this problem I brown my meat a few pieces at a time in hot oil and set them aside. Once I have made the sauce, I add the browned meat cubes (and all the good juices that come out of them) and let them cook.

These are just a few of the techniques that we use in Indian cookery. Others, that have to do with cooking rice or pulses, I shall deal with in later chapters.

MENUS AND
HOW TO EAT
INDIAN FOOD

What do you eat with what?

With each recipe in this book, I have suggested a menu. You do not have to follow it. After all, the fun of eating is to follow your own palate and put together dishes that are convenient and exciting for you.

Generally speaking, an Indian meal consists of a meat dish, a vegetable dish, bread and/or rice, a pulse dish, a yoghurt relish (or plain yoghurt), and a fresh chutney or small, relish-like salad. Pickles and preserved chutneys may be added if you have them. Fruit, rather than desserts are served at the end of a meal, although on festive occasions, sweets would not be at all amiss. Sometimes, when the meat dish is particularly elegant and rich, we eliminate the pulse and serve an equally elegant *pullao* rice. Vegetarians – of whom there are millions in India – increase the number of vegetable and pulse dishes and always serve yoghurt in some form.

Within this general framework, we try to see that the dishes we serve vary in colour, texture, and flavour. If the meat, for example, has a lot of sauce, then we often serve a 'dry', unsauced vegetable with it. If the vegetable we are serving is very soft – such as spinach – we make sure that there is a crunchy relish around on the table.

Most Indians like to eat with their hands. The more Westernised ones may use knives and forks or spoons and forks, or just forks, but they too succumb every now and then to the pleasure of eating with their fingers.

It is only the right hand that is used for eating, the left being considered 'unclean'. With it, we break pieces of bread and then use the pieces to scoop up some meat or vegetable. With it, we also form neat morsels out of rice and other accompanying dishes and then transport them to our mouths. In the northern states such as Uttar Pradesh, this is done very delicately with just the tips of the fingers. In the south, almost the entire hand may be used. Needless to say, hands must be washed before and after eating. Even the humblest of roadside stalls catering to simple villagers and truck drivers would not consider offering food before offering a *lota* (water vessel) of water for washing first.

When we serve ourselves, we put most foods beside each other on our plates. Only very wet, flowing dishes are sometimes ladled on top of the rice but not on top of *all* the rice. Some of the rice is left plain to enable us to eat it with other dishes. Very wet dishes that are meant to be eaten with bread are served in small, individual bowls.

OPPOSITE PAGE:

Sweet and sour okra, *Kutchhi bhindi* (page 112)
Gujerati carrot salad, *Gajar ka salad* (page 170)
Moghlai rice and lamb casserole, *Mughlai biryani* (page 154)

This is all very well if you are cooking a whole Indian meal. If you feel like making such a meal, then by all means, do it. On the other hand, there is no reason why you cannot serve an Indian vegetable with your roast lamb or eat an Indian meat (such as 'Chicken in a butter sauce', page 70) with French bread and a salad. If you are on a diet, you could make yourself a 'Yoghurt with cucumber and fresh mint' (page 162) for lunch and follow it with a crunchy apple. I have even served a roast leg of lamb with 'Black-eyed beans and mushrooms' (page 128), 'Simple buttery rice with onions' (page 149), and a green salad. It is an easy meal to put together *and* it is good.

The colour photographs in this book show combinations of recipes to serve together for a variety of meals. Here are some more menus:

Muglai lamb with turnips, *Shabdeg* (page 55)
Mushroom pullao, *Khumbi pullao* (page 152)
Spicy green beans, *Masaledar sem* (page 103)
Yoghurt with cucumber and mint, *Kheere ka raita* (page 162)

Prawns in a dark sauce, *Rasedar jhinga* (page 91)
Plain basmati rice, *Basmati chaaval* (page 147)
Cauliflower and potatoes, *Phool gobi aur aloo ki bhaji* (page 109)
Tomato, onion and green coriander relish, *Cachumber* (page 172)

Black eyed beans with mushrooms, *Lobhia aur khumbi* (page 128)
Cauliflower with onion and tomato, *Phool gobi ki bhaji* (page 108)
Layered bread, *Parathas* (page 138)
Gujerati carrot salad, *Gajar ka salad* (page 170)

OPPOSITE PAGE:
Sweet yellow rice, *Meetha pullao* (page 157) decorated with vark
Gujerati-style green beans, *Gujerati sem* (page 102)
Whole leg of lamb in a spicy yoghurt sauce, *Raan masaledar* (page 57)

Beef baked with yoghurt and black pepper, *Dum gosht* (page 50)
Aubergine cooked in the pickling style, *Baigan achari* (page 100)
Rice with peas, *Tahiri* (page 149)
Tomato, onion and green coriander relish, *Cachumber* (page 172)

Cod steaks in a spicy tomato sauce, *Timatar wali macchi* (page 95)
South Indian-style light, fluffy rice, *Dakshini chaaval* (page 147)
Spicy cucumber wedges, *Kheere ke tukray* (page 172)

EQUIPMENT

If you are going to cook authentic Indian food, do you need any special kitchen equipment?

For those of you who already have a well equipped kitchen, the answer is probably 'no'. Good knives, sturdy pots with a good distribution of heat, rolling pins, graters, bowls, slotted spoons, pestle and mortar, frying pans – I am sure you have these already.

There are, however, a few items that make the cooking of Indian food simpler.

An electric food processor or blender

Every Indian home has a grinding stone. This consists of a large flat stone that just sits and a smaller stone that is moved manually on top of it and does the actual grinding. These stones are exceedingly heavy. It is just as well that they are no longer essential. Their place, in modern kitchens, can be taken by food processors and blenders. Onions, garlic and ginger, formerly ground on grinding stones, can now be made into a paste in electrically powered machines.

If you do not have a food processor or blender, then there are ways around it. Garlic, for example, may be mashed in a mortar or put through a garlic press. Ginger may be grated on the finest part of the grater. Onions can just be chopped very finely. Sometimes my recipe suggests putting water into the food processor while making the paste. If you have crushed the garlic and grated the ginger by hand, just put them into a bowl and add the amount of water in the recipe.

If you decide to go out and buy a blender, make sure that its blades sit close to the bottom. Otherwise it will not pulverise small quantities adequately.

An electric coffee grinder

Food processors and blenders cannot do all the work of an Indian grinding stone. Dry spices, for example, cannot be ground in them properly. For this, only a coffee-grinder will do. A coffee-grinder grinds spices in seconds and can then be wiped clean. If you do not have one, you will have to crush your spices in small quantities with a pestle and mortar.

Tongs

My favourite tongs are intended for barbecues but I use them for turning chicken pieces, picking up meat pieces when they are browning, and even for tossing a salad.

A large non-stick frying pan with a lid

Non-stick pans really take the worry out of cooking many foods. Browning meats do not stick to the bottom, nor do sauces with ginger or almonds. As metal spoons ruin the finish of non-stick utensils, it is best to have a set of plastic or wooden ones.

Small and large cast-iron frying pans

I keep a 5 inch (13 cm) cast-iron frying pan for roasting spices – it can heat without oil or water in it – and for doing *baghaar*, frying small amounts of spices in oil. A larger cast-iron pan is excellent for making Indian breads such as *parathas* and *chapatis*. In India, these breads are cooked on a *tava*, a round, concave cast-iron plate. A large cast-iron frying pan makes the best substitute.

Karhai

This is very similar to a Chinese wok. If you took a large, hollow ball and cut it into half, that would be about the shape of a karhai. I am not suggesting that you go out and buy a karhai. I just wish to point out that for deep-frying, it is perhaps the most economical utensil as it allows you to use a relatively small quantity of oil while giving you enough depth in the centre of the utensil to submerge foods. A deep frying pan can be substituted for a karhai.

Electric Rice Cookers

If you frequently cook large quantities of rice, an electric rice cooker can be a useful piece of equipment. The cooker has a large covered pan which sits on top of an electric element. When the water has been absorbed by the rice, the cooker switches itself off, and will then keep the rice warm for several hours. The preparation of the rice and the amount of water you use are identical to the conventional methods of cooking rice (see page 144).

MEAT

This chapter has a great variety of meat dishes in it, going from *Kheema matar* 'Minced lamb with peas' and 'Pork chops with chickpeas' that you may wish to cook for your family, to *Raan masaledar* – a whole leg of lamb garnished with almonds and raisins – which would impress the most blasé of guests.

There are a lot of lamb recipes. We do eat a fair amount of lamb in India. We also eat a lot of goat. As goat is hard to find in Britain, I have substituted lamb in its place. I love English lamb. I realise that it is a bit expensive but it does have excellent flavour.

I find that the best cuts of lamb for stewing come from the neck and shoulder. Butchers have a way of trying to sell leg of lamb for stewing, mainly because it is easier to cut up. If you can, insist upon shoulder. You could buy a whole shoulder and carve up the meat yourself. Or you could buy shoulder chops and cut them up with a heavy cleaver. There is a lot of connective tissue in the shoulder and neck. This eventually makes for a moister meat.

In India, we usually leave the bone in the meat when we are cooking any stew-type dish. In fact, we throw in a few extra marrow bones for good measure because they affect the taste and texture of the sauce. As children, we always fought for the marrow bones. The victor not only got to eat the marrow but to use the funny, long, silver marrow spoons that sat decoratively in the centre of our dining table.

Many recipes in this book call for boned lamb. This is only because, over the years, I have seen many guests struggle with bones and have come to the conclusion that just because I like bones (I suck them), there is no reason to inflict them upon my guests. A majority of people who dine in our house seem to prefer boned meat. I leave the bone-in or bone-out decision up to you. Just remember that bones in stewing meat such as shoulder make up about 40 per cent of the total volume. If my recipe is for boned meat and you decide to leave the bone in, you might feed just half the number of people.

In India, we frequently cook meat with vegetables such as potatoes and turnips. The vegetables absorb the taste of the meat and lend their own flavour to the sauce.

I have included a few recipes for beef and pork as there are many communities in India which eat them. I, for one, simply love the beef baked with yoghurt and black pepper as well as the spicy and sour pork Vindaloo, a Goan speciality from India's west coast.

Minced lamb with mint

Pudine wala kheema

This dish, with its refreshing minty flavour, may be served very simply with rice, a pulse (such as 'Whole green lentils with spinach and ginger', page 125) and a yoghurt relish.

I often use it to stuff tomatoes in the summer. If you wish to do this, get firm, good-sized tomatoes and slice off a cap at the top. Scoop out the inside without breaking the skin and then season the inside of the tomato generously with salt and pepper. Stuff it loosely with the mince, put the caps back on and bake the tomatoes in a gas mark 6, 400 °F (200 °C) oven for about 15 minutes or until the skin just begins to crinkle. Serve with rice and a salad.

Serves 6:

- 6 oz (175g) onions, peeled
- 8–9 cloves garlic, peeled
- A 2 inch by 1 inch (5cm by 2.5cm) piece of fresh ginger, peeled and coarsely chopped
- 2 tablespoons ground cumin seeds
- 3 tablespoons water
- 4 teaspoons ground coriander seeds
- 1 teaspoon ground turmeric
- $\frac{1}{4}$–1 teaspoon cayenne pepper
- 4 tablespoons vegetable oil
- 4 whole cardamom pods
- 6 whole cloves
- 2 lb (900g) minced lamb
- About $1\frac{1}{2}$ teaspoons salt
- 2 oz (50g) finely chopped fresh mint leaves
- $\frac{1}{4}$ teaspoon garam masala (page 18)
- $1\frac{1}{2}$ tablespoons lemon juice

Chop half the onions finely and set them aside. Chop the other half coarsely and put them, along with the garlic, ginger, and 3 tablespoons water into the container of an electric blender. Blend until you have a smooth paste. Empty the paste into a small bowl. Add the cumin, coriander, turmeric and cayenne. Mix.

Heat the oil in a 10 inch (25cm) frying pan over a high flame. When hot, put in the cardamom and cloves. Two seconds later, put in the finely chopped onions. Stir and fry them until they turn fairly brown. Turn the heat to medium and put in the spice mixture from the small bowl. Stir and fry for 3–4 minutes. If the spice mixture sticks to the pan, sprinkle in a tablespoon of water and keep frying.

Put in the minced meat. Break up all the lumps and stir the mince about until it loses all its pinkness. Stir and fry another minute after that. Add the salt and mix. Cover, turn heat to very low and let the mince cook in its own juices for 25 minutes. Remove the cover and spoon off most of the accumulated fat. Add the chopped mint, *garam masala*, and lemon juice. Stir to mix and bring to a simmer. Cover, and simmer on very low heat for 3 minutes.

N.B. The whole cardamom and cloves in this dish are not meant to be eaten.

Minced meat with peas

Kheema matar

I associate this dish with very pleasurable family picnics which we had, sometimes in the private compartments of slightly sooty, steam-engined trains, and sometimes in the immaculate public gardens of historic Moghul palaces. The mince, invariably at room temperature, was eaten with *pooris* or *parathas* that had been stacked tightly in aluminium containers. There was always a pickle, to perk things up, and some kind of onion relish as well.

Serves 4–6:

4 tablespoons vegetable oil

3 oz (75g) onion, peeled and finely chopped

6–7 medium-sized cloves garlic peeled and finely chopped

1½ lb (700g) minced lamb (minced beef may be substituted)

A 1 inch cube of fresh ginger, peeled and grated to a pulp

1–2 fresh, hot green chillies, minced

1 teaspoon ground coriander seeds

1 teaspoon ground cumin seeds

$\frac{1}{8}$–$\frac{1}{4}$ teaspoon cayenne pepper

½ pint (275ml) water

6–7 oz (175–200g) shelled peas

4–6 heaped tablespoons chopped, fresh green coriander

About 1¼ teaspoon salt

1 teaspoon garam masala (page 18)

About 1½ tablespoons lemon juice

Heat the oil in a wide, medium-sized pan over a medium-high flame. When hot, put in the onions. Stir and fry them until they are lightly browned. Add the garlic. Stir and fry for another minute. Now put in the mince, ginger, green chillies, ground coriander seeds, cumin and cayenne. Stir and fry the meat for 5 minutes, breaking up lumps as you do so. Add 6 fl oz (175ml) of the water and bring to a boil. Cover, turn heat to low, and simmer for 30 minutes.

Add the peas, fresh coriander, salt, *garam masala*, lemon juice, and the remaining 4 fl oz (100ml) water. Mix and bring to a simmer. Cover and cook on low heat another 10 minutes or until peas are tender. Taste seasonings and adjust balance of salt and lemon juice if you need to.

A lot of fat might have collected at the bottom of your pan. Whenever you get ready to serve, lift the mince and peas out of the fat with a slotted spoon. Do not serve the fat.

Kashmiri meatballs

Kashmiri koftas

These sausage-shaped 'meatballs' taste very Kashmiri in their final blend of flavours. I often serve them with 'Plain basmati rice' (page 147), 'Red split lentils' (page 122), and 'Carrot and onion salad' (page 171).

Serves 6:

2 lb (900g) minced lamb

A piece of fresh ginger, about 1½ inches (4cm) long and 1 inch (2.5cm) thick, peeled and finely grated

1 tablespoon ground cumin seeds

1 tablespoon ground coriander seeds

¼ teaspoon ground cloves

¼ teaspoon ground cinnamon

⅛ teaspoon grated nutmeg

¼ teaspoon freshly ground black pepper

⅛–¼ teaspoon cayenne pepper

About 1¼ teaspoons salt

5 tablespoons plain yoghurt

7–8 tablespoons vegetable oil

A 2 inch (2.5cm) stick of cinnamon

5–6 whole cardamom pods

2 bay leaves

5–6 whole cloves

8 fl oz (225ml) warm water

Combine the lamb, ginger, cumin, coriander, ground cloves, ground cinnamon, grated nutmeg, black pepper, cayenne, salt and 3 tablespoons of the yoghurt in a bowl. Mix well.

Wet your hands with cold water and form 24 long *koftas* – sausage shapes, about 2½–3 (6–7.5cm) inches long and about 1 inch (2.5cm) thick.

Heat the oil in a large, preferably non-stick frying pan (or use two frying pans). When hot, put in the cinnamon stick, cardamom pods, bay leaves and whole cloves. Stir for a second. Now put in the *koftas* in a single layer and fry them on medium-high heat until they are lightly browned on all sides. Beat the remaining yoghurt into the 8 fl oz (225ml) warm water. Pour this over the *koftas* and bring to a boil. Cover, lower heat and simmer for about half an hour, turning the *koftas* around gently every 7–8 minutes. By the end of the half hour, no liquid other than the fat should be left in the frying pan. If necessary, turn up the heat to achieve this.

When you get ready to serve, lift the *koftas* out of the fat with a slotted spoon. Leave the whole spices behind as well.

Lamb with onions

Do piaza

This is an elegant dish that may be made as mild or as hot as you like. It is cooked with a fair amount of oil but most of this is skimmed off the top before serving. There are some whole spices in it – cloves, cardamom and cinnamon – which are not meant to be eaten. They should be pushed to the side as and when you come across them on your plates.

Lamb with onions may be served with rice or a bread. 'Spicy green beans' (page 103) also go well with it.

Serves 6:

4 good-sized onions, peeled

7 cloves garlic, peeled

A 1 inch (2.5cm) cube of fresh ginger, coarsely chopped

$\frac{3}{4}$ pint (425ml) water

10 tablespoons vegetable oil

A 1 inch (2.5cm) stick of cinnamon

10 whole cardamom pods

10 whole cloves

$2\frac{1}{2}$ lb (1kg 125g) boned lamb, preferably from the shoulder, cut into 1 inch (2.5cm) cubes (with most of the fat removed)

1 tablespoon ground coriander seeds

2 teaspoons ground cumin seeds

6 tablespoons plain yoghurt, beaten lightly

$\frac{1}{4}$–$\frac{1}{2}$ teaspoon cayenne pepper

About $1\frac{1}{4}$ teaspoons salt

$\frac{1}{2}$ teaspoon garam masala (page 18)

Cut three of the onions into halves, lengthwise and then cut them, crosswise, into very fine half rings. Chop the fourth onion finely. Keep the two types of onion separate.

Put the garlic and ginger into the container of an electric blender or food processor. Add 4 fl oz (100ml) of the measured water and blend until fairly smooth.

Heat the oil in a wide, heavy saucepan over a medium-high flame. When hot, put in the finely sliced onions. Stir and fry for 10–12 minutes or until the onions turn a nice, reddish-brown colour. You may have to turn the heat down somewhat towards the end of this cooking period. Remove the onions with a slotted spoon and spread them on a plate lined with paper towels (or clean brown paper).

Put the cinnamon, cardamom and cloves into the hot oil. Stir them about for about 5 seconds over medium-high heat. Now put in 8–10 cubes of meat or as many as the saucepan will hold easily in a single, loosely packed layer. Brown the meat on one side. Turn it over and brown the opposite side. Remove the meat cubes with a slotted spoon and put them in a bowl. Brown all the meat this way, removing each batch as it gets done.

Put the chopped onion into the remaining oil in the saucepan. Stir and fry it on medium heat until the pieces turn brown at the edges. Add the garlic-ginger paste. Stir and fry it until all the water in it seems to boil away and you see the oil again. Turn the heat down a bit and add the coriander and cumin. Stir and fry for 30 seconds. Now add 1 tablespoon of the yoghurt. Stir and fry until it is incorporated into the sauce. Add another tablespoon of yoghurt. Stir and fry, incorporating this into the sauce as well. Add all the yoghurt this way, a tablespoon at a time. Now put in all the meat and any accumulated juices in the meat bowl with the remaining water, the cayenne and the salt. Stir to mix and bring to a simmer. Cover, turn heat to low and cook for about 45 minutes or until the lamb is tender. Add the fried onions and the *garam masala*. Stir to mix. Cook, uncovered, for another 2–3 minutes, stirring gently as you do so.

Turn off the heat and let the pan sit for a while. The fat will rise to the top. Remove it with a spoon.

N.B. This dish may be prepared ahead of time and reheated.

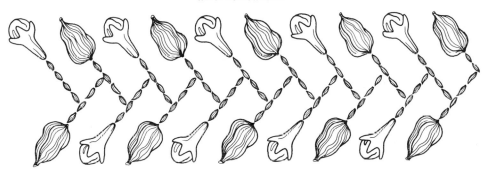

Kashmiri lamb stew

Kashmiri yakhni

Some Kashmiri dishes are fiercely hot, others mild and soothing. Often, they are served together at the same meal. For those of you who are unused to very spicy foods, this might be the perfect dish to try first. It is really a lamb stew – with lots of lovely fennel flavour but no hot chillies – that is eventually thickened with yoghurt so it has a creamy tartness. You could serve it with plain rice, as Kashmiris do.

Serves 4–6:

4 teaspoons whole fennel seeds
6 tablespoons vegetable oil or ghee
A pinch of ground asafetida, optional
3 lb (1kg 350g) shoulder of lamb boned or unboned, cut roughly into 2 inch (5cm) cubes
A 1 inch (2.5cm) stick of cinnamon
10 whole cardamom pods
15 whole cloves
1¾ teaspoons salt – or to taste
1½ pints (845ml) water
1½ teaspoons dried ginger powder
15 fl oz (425ml) plain yoghurt
¼ teaspoon garam masala (page 18)

Put the fennel seeds into a clean coffee grinder or other spice grinder and grind until you have a powder.

Heat the oil in a heavy, wide pot over high heat. When hot, put in the asafetida. One second later, put in all the meat, as well as the cinnamon, cardamom, cloves and salt. Stir and cook, uncovered, over high heat for about 5 minutes or until almost all the water released by the meat disappears and the meat browns very lightly. Lower the heat to medium and add 1 tablespoon water, the fennel and ginger. Stir to mix. Add 1½ pints (845ml) water, cover partially, and simmer on medium heat for 30 minutes. Cover completely, turn heat to low and simmer for 40 minutes or until the meat is tender. Stir a few times as the meat cooks, adding a few tablespoons of water if it seems to dry out.

Beat the yoghurt in a bowl until it is smooth and creamy.

Remove the cover from the meat pot and turn the heat to medium-low. Push the meat cubes to the edges of the pot, leaving a well-like space in the centre. Pour the yoghurt very slowly into this well, while moving a slotted spoon back and forth quite fast in the same area. (If you do not do this, the yoghurt will curdle.) Keep up the back and forth movement of the slotted spoon for a good 5 minutes *after* all the yoghurt has been poured in. You should now have a simmering, creamy sauce. Cover partially and continue to cook on medium-low heat for another 10 minutes. Sprinkle in the *garam masala* and mix.

N.B. The whole spices in the stew are not meant to be eaten.

Lamb with spinach

Dilli ka saag gosht

This dish could also be made with beef. Use cubed chuck steak and cook it for about 2 hours or until it is tender. Dilli ka saag gosht may be served with rice or bread. I think 'Fried aubergine slices' (page 99) and a yoghurt dish would complement the meat well.

Serves 6:

8 tablespoons vegetable oil

¼ teaspoon whole black peppercorns

6–7 whole cloves

2 bay leaves

6 cardamom pods

6 oz (175g) onions, peeled and finely chopped

6–8 cloves garlic, peeled and finely chopped

A 1 inch (2.5cm) cube of ginger, peeled and finely chopped

2 lb (900g) boned meat from lamb shoulder, cut into 1 inch (2.5cm) cubes

2 teaspoons ground cumin seeds

1 teaspoon ground coriander seeds

¼–¾ teaspoon cayenne pepper

2 teaspoons salt

5 tablespoons plain yoghurt, well beaten

2 lb (900g) fresh spinach, trimmed, washed and finely chopped or 2 lb (900g) frozen spinach, thawed out, may be substituted

¼ teaspoon garam masala (page 18)

Heat the oil in a large pot over a medium-high flame. When hot, put in the peppercorns, cloves, bay leaves, and cardamom pods. Stir for a second. Now put in the onions, garlic, and ginger. Stir and fry until the onions develop brown specks. Now add the meat, ground cumin, ground coriander, cayenne pepper, and 1 teaspoon of the salt. Stir and fry for a minute. Add 1 tablespoon of the beaten yoghurt. Stir and fry for another minute. Add another tablespoon of the yoghurt. Stir and fry for a minute. Keep doing this until all the yoghurt has been incorporated. The meat should also have a slightly browned look. Add the spinach and the remaining 1 teaspoon salt. Stir to mix. Keep stirring and cooking until the spinach wilts completely. Cover tightly and simmer on low heat for about 1 hour 10 minutes or until meat is tender.

Remove the lid and add the *garam masala*. Turn the heat to medium. Stir and cook another 5 minutes or until most (but not all) the water in the spinach disappears and you have a thick, green sauce.

N.B. The whole spices in this dish are not meant to be eaten.

Beef baked with yoghurt and black pepper

Dum gosht

Ever since the Moghuls came to India, there has been a method of cooking that Indians refer to as '*dum*'. Meat (or rice for that matter) is partially cooked in a heavy pot and then covered over with a flat lid. At this stage the pot and lid are sealed with a 'rope' made out of very stiff dough. The pot is placed over a gentle fire – generally the last of the charcoals – and more hot charcoals are spread over the lid. The meat proceeds to cook very slowly until it is tender, often in small amounts of liquid.

In today's world, this *dum* method of cooking is the equivalent of slow oven baking. So what I have done here is to update a very traditional, top-of-the-cooker, Moghul recipe, modernising it just enough to suit our contemporary kitchens. As with many other *dum* foods, this is not a dish with a lot of sauce. Ideally, whatever sauce there is should be thick and cling to the meat.

If you like, you could leave out the cayenne in this recipe. That is probably what the early Moghuls did. The later Moghuls, seduced by the chilli peppers brought over from the New World by the Portuguese, used it generously.

I love to eat this meat dish with *chapatis* or *parathas* or *naans*. If you prefer rice, then the more moist pullaos, such as 'Mushroom pullao' (page 152), would be the perfect accompaniment.

You could also make this dish with stewing lamb meat from the shoulder.

Serves 4–6:

6 tablespoons vegetable oil
2 lb (900g) boneless stewing beef from the neck and shoulder, cut into 1½ inch (4cm) cubes
½ lb (225g) onions, peeled and very finely chopped
6 cloves garlic, peeled and very finely chopped
½ teaspoon dried, powdered ginger
⅛–½ teaspoon cayenne pepper
1 tablespoon paprika
2 teaspoons salt
½ teaspoon very coarsely ground black pepper
10 fl oz (275ml) plain yoghurt, beaten lightly

Preheat oven to gas mark 4 or 350 °F (180 °C).

Heat the oil in a wide, flameproof casserole-type pot over a medium-high flame. When hot, put in as many meat pieces as the pot will hold easily in a single layer. Brown the meat pieces on all sides and set them aside in a deep plate. Brown all the meat this way.

Put the onions and garlic into the same pot and turn the heat down to medium. Stir and fry the onion-garlic mixture for about 10 minutes or until it has browned. Now put in the browned meat as well as any juices that might have accumulated in the plate. Also put in the ginger, cayenne, paprika, salt, and pepper. Stir for a minute. Now put in the yoghurt and bring to a simmer. Cover tightly, first with aluminium foil and then with a lid, and bake in the oven for 1½ hours. The meat should be tender by now. If it is not tender, pour in 5 fl oz (150ml) of boiling water, cover tightly, and bake another 20–30 minutes or until meat is tender. Stir meat gently before serving.

Red lamb or beef stew

Rogan josh

Rogan josh gets its name from its rich, red appearance. The red appearance, in turn, is derived from ground red chillies, which are used quite generously in this recipe. If you want your dish to have the right colour and not be very hot, combine paprika with cayenne pepper in any proportion that you like. Just make sure that your paprika is fresh and has a good red colour. There are many recipes for *rogan josh*. This is probably the simplest of them all. It may be served with an Indian bread or rice. A green bean or aubergine dish would be a perfect accompaniment.

Serves 4–6:

Two 1 inch (2.5cm) cubes of fresh ginger, peeled and coarsely chopped

8 cloves garlic, peeled

4 tablespoons plus $\frac{1}{2}$–$\frac{3}{4}$ pint (275–425ml) water

10 tablespoons vegetable oil

2 lb (900g) boned meat from lamb shoulder or leg, or stewing beef (chuck), cut into 1 inch (2.5cm) cubes

10 whole cardamom pods

2 bay leaves

6 whole cloves

10 whole peppercorns

A 1 inch (2.5cm) stick of cinnamon

7 oz (200g) onions, peeled and finely chopped

1 teaspoon ground coriander seeds

2 teaspoons ground cumin seeds

4 teaspoons bright red paprika mixed with $\frac{1}{4}$–1 teaspoon cayenne pepper

$1\frac{1}{4}$ teaspoons salt

6 tablespoons plain yoghurt

$\frac{1}{4}$ teaspoon garam masala (page 18)

Freshly ground black pepper

Put the ginger, garlic, and 4 tablespoons water into the container of an electric blender. Blend well until you have a smooth paste.

Heat the oil in a wide, heavy pot over a medium-high flame. Brown the meat cubes in several batches and set to one side. Put the cardamom, bay leaves, cloves, peppercorns, and cinnamon into the same hot oil. Stir once and wait until the cloves swell and the bay leaves begin to take on colour. This just takes a few seconds. Now put in the onions. Stir and fry for about 5 minutes or until the onions turn a medium-brown colour. Put in the ginger-garlic paste and stir for 30 seconds. Then add the coriander, cumin, paprika-cayenne, and salt. Stir and fry for another 30 seconds. Add the fried meat cubes and juices. Stir for 30 seconds. Now put in 1 tablespoon of the yoghurt. Stir and fry for about 30 seconds or until the yoghurt is well blended. Add the remaining yoghurt, a tablespoon at a time, in the same way. Stir and fry for another 3–4 minutes.

Now add $\frac{1}{2}$ pint (275ml) of water if you are cooking lamb and $\frac{3}{4}$ pint (425ml) water if you are cooking beef. Bring the contents of the pot to a boil, scraping in all browned spices on the sides and bottom of the pot. Cover, turn heat to low and simmer for about an hour if you are cooking lamb and 2 hours if you are cooking beef, or until meat is tender. (The meat could also be baked, covered in a preheated gas mark 4, 350°F (180°C) oven for the same length of time or until tender.) Every 10 minutes or so, give the meat a good stir. When the meat is tender, take off the lid, turn the heat up to medium, and boil away some of the liquid. You should end up with tender meat in a thick, reddish-brown sauce. All the fat that collects in the pot may be spooned off the top Sprinkle the *garam masala* and black pepper over the meat before you serve and mix them in.

Kashmiri red lamb stew

Kashmiri rogan josh

Kashmiri Hindus do not eat any onions or garlic and they often use dry, powdered ginger instead of the fresh kind. This is their very different and quite delicious version of *rogan josh*. (For more on *rogan josh*, see the introduction to the preceding recipe.) I have left the bones in the meat this time as most Indians really prefer their meat this way. *Kashmiri rogan josh* may be served with 'Frozen spinach with potatoes' (page 116), plain long-grain rice and a relish.

Serves 4–6:

1 tablespoon whole fennel seeds

25 fl oz (720ml) plain yoghurt

6 tablespoons vegetable oil

A $\frac{3}{4}$ inch (2cm) stick of cinnamon

$\frac{1}{2}$ teaspoon whole cloves

A pinch of ground asafetida, optional

3 lb (1kg 350g) stewing meat (with bone) from lamb shoulder and neck, cut into 2 inch (5cm) cubes

$2\frac{1}{2}$ teaspoons salt – or to taste

4 teaspoons bright red paprika mixed with $\frac{1}{4}$–1 teaspoon cayenne pepper

$1\frac{1}{2}$ teaspoons dried ginger powder

$1\frac{1}{2}$ pints (845ml) water

$\frac{1}{4}$ teaspoon garam masala (page 18)

Put the fennel seeds into the container of a spice grinder or clean coffee grinder and grind until fine.

Put the yoghurt in a bowl and beat it with a fork or a whisk until it is smooth and creamy.

Heat the oil in a large pot over a high flame. When hot, put in the cinnamon and cloves. A second later, put in the ground asafetida. A second after that, put in all the meat and the salt. Stir the meat and cook, still on a high flame, for about 5 minutes. Now put in the paprika and cayenne and give the meat a good stir. Slowly add the yoghurt, 4–5 fl oz (100–150ml) at a time stirring the meat vigorously as you do so. Add all the yoghurt this way. Keep cooking on high heat until all the liquid has boiled away and the meat pieces have browned slightly. Add the fennel and ginger. Give the meat some more good stirs. Now put in $1\frac{1}{2}$ pints (845ml) water, cover so as to leave the lid very slightly ajar, and cook on medium heat for 30 minutes. Cover completely and cook on low heat for another 45 minutes or until meat is tender. Stir a few times as the meat cooks, making sure that there is always some liquid in the pot.

Remove the lid and add the *garam masala*. You should have a thick reddish brown sauce. If it is too thin boil some of the liquid away.

Delhi-style lamb cooked with potatoes

Aloo gosht

This is one of the everyday meat dishes that I grew up with in Delhi. I still love its homey taste and have a particular weakness for its sauce, which seems to combine all the goodness of lamb, potatoes, tomatoes, and the cheaper, commoner Indian spices – cumin, coriander, turmeric, and cayenne pepper. I like it with rice or an Indian bread and 'Gujerati-style green beans' (page 102).

Serves 6:

7 tablespoons vegetable oil

6 oz (175g) onions, peeled and finely chopped

$\frac{1}{2}$–1 fresh green chilli, finely chopped

5 cloves garlic, peeled and finely chopped

$2\frac{1}{4}$ lb (1kg) boned lamb meat from the shoulder, cut into 1 inch (2.5cm) cubes

12 oz (350g) fresh tomatoes, peeled (see page 29) and finely chopped (tinned tomatoes may be substituted)

1 tablespoon ground cumin seeds

2 teaspoons ground coriander seeds

$\frac{1}{2}$ teaspoon ground turmeric

$\frac{1}{4}$–1 teaspoon cayenne pepper

2 teaspoons salt

1 lb (450g) medium-sized potatoes, peeled and cut into half

$1\frac{1}{2}$ pints (845ml) water

Heat the oil in a large, heavy pot over a high flame. When hot, put in the onions, green chilli, and garlic. Stir and fry until the onions have browned slightly. Put in the meat and stir it about vigorously for about 5 minutes. Now put in the tomatoes, cumin, coriander, turmeric, cayenne pepper and salt. Continue to stir and cook on high heat for 10–15 minutes or until the sauce is thick and the oil seems to separate from it. Add the potatoes and $1\frac{1}{2}$ pints (845ml) water. Cover, leaving the lid just very slightly ajar, and cook on medium-low heat for about 1 hour 10 minutes or until the meat is tender and the sauce is thick.

Mughlai lamb with turnips
Shabdeg

Turnips are perhaps the most under-rated vegetable in the world. This classical Moghul recipe calls for small, whole turnips. The turnips end up by absorbing all the delicious meat juices, turning buttery soft and yet retaining their own rather pretty shape. I like to serve this dish with 'Mushroom pullao' (page 152) and 'Spicy green beans' (page 103). *Dal* and a yoghurt relish can also be added to the meal.

Serves 6:

10 small turnips, weighing 1½ lb (700g) without leaves and stems (if your turnips are larger, halve them)

2¾ teaspoons salt

1 lb (450g) onions, peeled

8 tablespoons vegetable oil

2¼ lb (1kg) stewing meat (with bone) from lamb shoulder, cut into 1½ inch (4cm) cubes

10 fl oz (275ml) plain yoghurt

A 1 inch piece of fresh ginger, peeled and very finely chopped

½ teaspoon ground turmeric

½ teaspoon cayenne pepper

1 tablespoon ground coriander seeds

4 pints (2.25 litres) water

½ teaspoon garam masala (page 18)

Peel the turnips and prick them all over with a fork. Put them in a bowl and rub them with ¾ teaspoon salt. Set aside for 1½–2 hours.

Cut the onions in half, lengthwise, and then crosswise into very thin slices.

Heat the oil in a large, wide, and preferably non-stick pot over a medium-high flame. When hot, put in the onions. Stir and fry for about 12 minutes or until the onions are a reddish-brown colour. Remove the onions with a slotted spoon, squeezing out and leaving behind as much oil as you can. Spread the onions out on a plate.

Put the meat into the same pot. Also put in the yoghurt, ginger and 1 teaspoon salt. Stir and bring to a boil. Turn the heat up high. You should, at this stage, have a fair amount of rather thin sauce. Cook on high heat, stirring every now and then, for about 10 minutes or until the sauce is fairly thick and you just begin to see the oil. Turn the heat down a bit to medium-high and continue to stir and fry for 5–7 minutes or until the meat is lightly browned and the sauce has disappeared. Turn the heat to medium-low. Put in the turmeric, cayenne, and ground coriander. Stir for a minute.

Now put in 4 pints (2.25 litres) water and 1 teaspoon salt. Drain the turnips and add them as well. Bring the pot to a boil. Turn the heat to medium-high and cook, uncovered, for about 45 minutes or until you have less than a third of the liquid left. Stir several times during this cooking period.

Put in the browned onions and the *garam masala*. Stir gently to mix and turn heat to low. Cook gently, uncovered, for another 10 minutes. Stir a few times during this period, taking care not to break the turnips.

Spoon off the oil that floats to the top and serve hot.

'Royal' lamb or beef with a creamy almond sauce
Shahi korma

There are many Indian dishes that were inspired, a few centuries ago, by dishes from other countries. *Shahi korma* – lamb cubes smothered in a rich almond and cream sauce – owes its ancestry to Persian food.

It could be served with rice (perhaps 'Spiced basmati rice', page 148) or a bread (*naan*, *chapati*, or *paratha*) and a vegetable such as 'Cauliflower with potatoes', (page 109). It would be good to have some kind of tomato or onion relish on the side. When I want a quick, but elegant, meal, I have been known to serve *shahi korma* with plain rice and a crisp green salad.

In my recipe here, I have cooked *shahi korma* the traditional way, that is on top of the cooker. If you like, you could do the final long cooking in the oven. This is particularly useful if you are making a large meal and need the top of the cooker for other dishes. Just preheat the oven to gas mark 4, 350°F (180°C) and, once you have combined the meat, salt, cream and water and brought it to a boil, you can cover the pot and put it in the oven instead. The cooking times and other general directions remain the same.

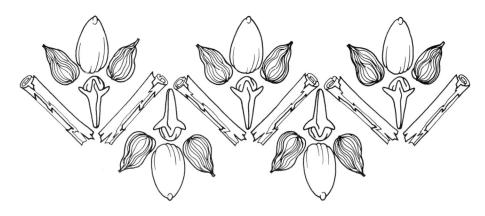

Serves 4–6:

8 cloves garlic, peeled

A 1 inch (2.5cm) cube of fresh ginger, peeled and coarsely chopped

2 oz (50g) blanched, slivered almonds

6 tablespoons plus 4–8 fl oz (100–225ml) water

7 tablespoons vegetable oil

2 lb (900g) boned lamb from the shoulder or leg or stewing beef (chuck), cut into 1 inch (2.5cm) cubes

10 whole cardamom pods

6 whole cloves

A 1 inch (2.5cm) stick of cinnamon

7 oz (200g) onions, peeled and finely chopped

1 teaspoon ground coriander seeds

2 teaspoons ground cumin seeds

$\frac{1}{2}$ teaspoon cayenne pepper

$1\frac{1}{4}$ teaspoons salt

$\frac{1}{2}$ pint (275ml) single cream

$\frac{1}{4}$ teaspoon garam masala (page 18)

Put the garlic, ginger, almonds, and 6 tablespoons of the water into the container of an electric blender. Blend until you have a paste.

Heat the oil in a wide, heavy, preferably non-stick pot over a medium-high flame. When hot, put in just enough meat pieces so they lie, uncrowded, in a single layer. Brown the meat pieces on all sides, then remove them with a slotted spoon and put them in a bowl. Brown all the meat this way.

Put the cardamom, cloves, and cinnamon into the hot oil. Within seconds the cloves will expand. Now put in the onions. Stir and fry the onions until they turn a brownish colour. Turn the heat down to medium. Put in the paste from the blender as well as the coriander, cumin, and cayenne. Stir and fry this mixture for 3–4 minutes or until it too has browned somewhat. Now put in the meat cubes as well as any liquid that might have accumulated in the meat bowl, the salt, the cream, and 4 fl oz (100ml) water. If you are cooking beef, add another 4 fl oz (100ml) water. Bring to a boil. Cover, turn heat to low and simmer lamb for 1 hour and beef for 2 hours or until the meat is tender. Stir frequently during this cooking period. Skim off any fat that floats to the top. Sprinkle in the *garam masala* and mix.

N.B. The whole spices in this dish are not meant to be eaten.

Whole leg of lamb in a spicy yoghurt sauce

Raan masaledar

If you are having guests for dinner, this might be the perfect dish to serve. It is quite impressive – a whole leg dressed with a rich sauce, served garnished with almonds and sultanas. I often serve it with 'Sweet yellow rice' (page 157) and a green vegetable.

You need to buy a 5 lb (2kg) leg of lamb. Get the butcher to remove the H bone and to make a deep pocket to hold a stuffing. (You will not actually stuff the leg but most butchers seem to understand 'stuffing' better than they do 'spice paste'.) Also, ask the butcher to cut the protruding leg bone as close to the end of the meat as possible. This is to enable you to fit it into your baking pan easily. Ask the butcher to remove all the fat on the outside of the leg as well as the parchment like skin. (You could, of course, do this yourself.)

For baking, you need a pan large enough to hold the leg easily and about $2-2\frac{1}{2}$ inches (5–6cm) deep to hold the sauce. Ideally, the pan should have a lid but you can use aluminium foil instead. Pyrex and stainless steel baking pans are best as they do not affect the taste of the sauce.

Serves 4–6:

A 5 lb (2.25kg) leg of lamb, trimmed (see above)

For the sauce:

2 oz (50g) blanched almonds

$\frac{1}{2}$ lb (225g) onions, peeled and coarsely chopped

8 cloves garlic, peeled

Four 1 inch (2.5cm) cubes of ginger, peeled and coarsely chopped

4 fresh hot green chillies, coarsely chopped

20 fl oz (570ml) plain yoghurt

2 tablespoons ground cumin seeds

4 teaspoons ground coriander seeds

$\frac{1}{2}$ teaspoon cayenne pepper

$3\frac{1}{2}$ teaspoons salt

$\frac{1}{2}$ teaspoon garam masala (page 18)

6 tablespoons vegetable oil

$\frac{1}{2}$ teaspoon whole cloves

16 cardamom pods

A 2 inch (5cm) stick of cinnamon

10 black peppercorns

Make sure that all the fat has been trimmed from the outside of the leg and that most of the fell (parchment-like white skin) has been pulled off. Put the leg in a baking dish made, preferably, of pyrex or stainless steel.

Put the 2 oz (50g) almonds, onions, garlic, ginger, green chillies, and 3 tablespoons of the yoghurt into the container of a food processor or blender and blend until you have a paste.

Put the remaining yoghurt into a bowl. Beat lightly with a fork or a whisk until it is smooth and creamy. Add the paste from the processor, the cumin, coriander, cayenne, salt, and *garam masala*. Mix.

Push some of the spice paste into all the openings in the lamb. Be quite generous about this. Spread the paste evenly on the underside of the leg (the side that originally had less fat). Now, using a small, sharp, pointed knife (such as a paring knife), make deep slashes in the meat and push in the spice paste with your fingers. Turn the leg over so its outer side (the side that was once covered with fat) is on top. Spread a very thick layer of paste over it. Again, make deep slashes with the knife and push the spice paste into the slashes. Pour all the remaining spice paste over and around the meat. Cover with plastic cling film and refrigerate for 24 hours.

For garnishing:

4 tablespoons sultanas

½ oz (10g) blanched, split or slivered almonds

Take the baking dish with the meat out of the refrigerator and let the meat come to room temperature. Remove the cling film. Heat the oil in a small frying pan over a medium flame. When hot, put in the cloves, cardamom, cinnamon and peppercorns. When the cloves swell – this just takes a few seconds – pour the hot oil and spices over the leg of lamb.

Preheat oven to gas mark 6, 400°F (200°C).

Cover the baking dish tightly either with its own lid or with a large piece of aluminium foil. Bake, covered, for 1 hour 30 minutes. Remove the foil and bake uncovered for 45 minutes. Baste 3–4 times with the sauce during this period. Scatter, or arrange in a pattern, the sultanas and the ½ oz (15g) almonds over the top of the leg and bake for another 5–6 minutes. Remove the baking dish from the oven and let it sit in a warm place for 15 minutes. Take the leg out of the pan and set it on a warm platter. Spoon off all the fat from the top of the sauce. Use a slotted spoon and fish out all the whole spices in the sauce. Discard the spices. Pour the sauce around the leg.

Goan-style hot and sour pork

Vindaloo

The Hindus and Muslims of India do not, generally, eat pork – but Indian Christians do. This dish, with its semi-Portuguese name suggesting that the meat is cooked with wine (or vinegar) and garlic, is a contribution from the Konkani-speaking Christians of western India.

Vindaloos, which may be made out of lamb and beef as well, are usually very, very hot. You can control this heat by putting in just as many red chillies as you think you can manage. Serve mounds of fluffy rice on the side.

Serves 6:

2 teaspoons whole cumin seeds

2–3 hot, dried red chillies

1 teaspoon black peppercorns

1 teaspoon cardamom seeds (you may take the seeds out of pods if you cannot buy them loose)

A 3 inch (2cm) stick of cinnamon

1½ teaspoons whole black mustard seeds

1 teaspoon whole fenugreek seeds

5 tablespoons white wine vinegar

1½–2 teaspoons salt

1 teaspoon light brown sugar

10 tablespoons vegetable oil

6–7 oz (175–200g) onions, peeled and sliced into fine half-rings

4–6 tablespoons plus 8 fl oz (225ml) water

2 lb (900g) boneless pork shoulder meat, cut into 1 inch (2.5cm) cubes

A 1 inch (2.5cm) cube of fresh ginger, peeled and coarsely chopped

A small, whole head of garlic, with all the cloves separated and peeled (or the equivalent, if using a large one)

1 tablespoon ground coriander seeds

½ teaspoon ground turmeric

Grind cumin seeds, red chillies, peppercorns, cardamom seeds, cinnamon, black mustard seeds and fenugreek seeds in a coffee-grinder or other spice grinder. Put the ground spices in a bowl. Add the vinegar, salt and sugar. Mix and set aside.

Heat the oil in a wide, heavy pot over a medium flame. Put in the onions. Fry, stirring frequently, until the onions turn brown and crisp. Remove the onions with a slotted spoon and put them into the container of an electric blender or food processor. (Turn the heat off.) Add 2–3 tablespoons of water to the blender and purée the onions. Add this purée to the ground spices in the bowl. (This is the *vindaloo* paste). It may be made ahead of time and frozen.)

Dry off the meat cubes with a paper towel and remove large pieces of fat, if any.

Put the ginger and garlic into the container of an electric blender or food processor. Add 2–3 tablespoons of water and blend until you have a smooth paste.

Heat the oil remaining in the pot once again over a medium-high flame. When hot, put in the pork cubes, a few at a time, and brown them lightly on all sides. Remove each batch with a slotted spoon and keep in a bowl. Do all the pork this way. Now put the ginger-garlic paste into the same pot. Turn down the heat to medium. Stir the paste for a few seconds. Add the coriander and turmeric. Stir for another few seconds. Add the meat, any juices that may have accumulated as well as the *vindaloo* paste and 8 fl oz (225ml) water. Bring to a boil. Cover and simmer gently for an hour or until pork is tender. Stir a few times during this cooking period.

Pork chipolatas cooked in an Indian style

Indians cannot, of course, buy chipolatas in their local bazaars but here is a simple Indian-style recipe that I use when I am rushed to get dinner on the table. 'Potatoes with black pepper' (page 113) may be served on the side.

Serves 4:

A 1 inch (2.5cm) cube of fresh ginger, peeled and coarsely chopped

3 cloves garlic, peeled

4 tablespoons water

½ lb (225g) small courgettes

2 tablespoons vegetable oil

½ lb (225g) pork chipolatas

4 oz (110g) onion, peeled and chopped

1 teaspoon ground cumin seeds

¼ teaspoon cayenne pepper

½ lb (225g) tomatoes, peeled (see page 29) and finely chopped (you may use an 8 oz (225g) can of tomatoes as a substitute)

½ teaspoon salt

Put the ginger, garlic, and 4 tablespoons water into the container of a food processor or blender. Blend until you have a paste.

Quarter the courgettes, lengthwise, and then cut the strips into 1½ inch (4cm) lengths.

Heat the oil in a large frying pan over a medium flame. Put in the chipolatas. Fry, turning the chipolatas whenever necessary, until they have browned on all sides. Remove and keep in a plate.

Put the onions into the same oil. Stir and fry until they begin to turn brown at the edges. Add the ginger-garlic paste. Stir and fry for a minute. Put in the cumin and cayenne. Stir a few times and put in the tomatoes. Stir for a minute. Put in the courgettes and salt. Bring to a simmer, cover, turn heat to low and cook for 10 minutes.

Cut the chipolatas into 3 pieces each. Add them to the pan. Cover and cook for about 5 minutes or until the chipolatas have heated through.

Pork chops with chickpeas
Chhole wala gosht

Normally, this hearty, stewtype dish is cooked with cubes of pork cut off from the shoulder. I have substituted the more easily available thin-cut pork chops and added some mushrooms for good measure.

In India, we often ate this dish with what was pronounced as 'selice' and was, in reality, *slices* of white bread. (As a child, I had assumed that 'selice' was just another Indian word!) I now prefer slices from the crustier French loaf. Beside the bread, you need to serve nothing more than a simple vegetable, cooked in an Indian or English style. A simple salad would also do.

This is a perfect dish for a winter's day and is best served in individual bowls or soup plates.

Dried chickpeas can be cooked in many ways. You can soak them overnight before cooking them or you can follow the method that I have used here which allows the entire dish to be made in the course of a single day.

You may make these pork chops a day ahead of time and just reheat them.

Serves 6:

$\frac{1}{2}$ lb (225g) dried chickpeas, picked over, rinsed, and drained

3 pints (1.75 litres) plus 3 tablespoons water

A 1$\frac{1}{2}$ inch (4cm) cube of fresh ginger, peeled and coarsely chopped

5 cloves garlic, peeled

4 tablespoons vegetable oil

2 lb (900g) thin-cut pork chops (sometimes called 'breakfast chops')

8 whole cardamom pods

A 1 inch (2.5cm) stick of cinnamon

2 bay leaves

1 teaspoon whole cumin seeds

6 oz (175g) onions, peeled and coarsely chopped

1 tablespoon ground cumin seeds

1 tablespoon ground coriander seeds

1 teaspoon ground turmeric

11 oz (300g) tomatoes, peeled (see page 29) and chopped

$\frac{3}{4}$ lb (350g) potatoes, peeled and cut into $\frac{3}{4}$ inch (2cm) dice

1 tablespoon salt

10 oz (275g) medium-sized mushrooms, halved

$\frac{1}{2}$ teaspoon cayenne pepper (use more or less as desired)

Put the chickpeas in a pot. Add 3 pints (1.75 litres) water and bring to a boil. Cover, turn heat to low and simmer 2 minutes. Turn off the heat and let the pot sit, covered, for 1 hour. Bring the chickpeas to a boil again. Cover, turn heat to low and simmer for 1$\frac{1}{2}$ hours.

Put the ginger, garlic, and 3 tablespoons water into the container of a food processor or blender. Blend until you have a paste.

Heat the oil in a large, wide pot over a medium-high flame. When hot, put in as many pork chops as the pot will hold in a single layer. Brown them on both sides without attempting to cook them through. Remove the chops and put them on a plate.

Put the cardamom, cinnamon, bay leaves, and whole cumin seeds into the hot oil. Immediately, turn the heat down to medium-low. Stir once and put in the onions. Stir and fry the onions for a minute, scraping the hardened pan juices as you do so. Now put in the ginger-garlic paste and stir once. Put in the ground cumin, coriander, and turmeric. Stir for a minute. Put in the tomatoes, potatoes, pork chops and any liquid that may have accumulated in the plate, salt, as well as the chickpeas and all their cooking liquid. Stir and bring to a boil. Cover, turn heat to low and simmer 45 minutes. Add the mushrooms and cayenne. Cover and simmer for 15 minutes.

N.B. The large whole spices in this dish should not be eaten.

CHICKEN

Since chicken is now mass produced – and fairly cheap, its status has been greatly reduced. This saddens me. I was brought up thinking of chicken as something special and have never managed to get over thinking so; besides, I like chicken. And there are such wonderful ways to cook it, from the simple 'Spicy baked chicken' to the elegant *Makkhani murghi* ('Chicken in a butter sauce') and the very impressive *Murgh musallam* ('Whole chicken baked in aluminium foil'). If you are on a diet, you can eat 'Tandoori chicken' which is cooked without fat and when you want to indulge yourself, you can dine on *Shahjahani murghi* ('Mughlai chicken with almonds and raisins').

There are two things to remember when cooking Indian-style chicken dishes. The first is that we nearly always skin the chicken before we cook it. Skin has never been popular in India, perhaps because it gets so soft and flabby in stews. The second is that, for most of our dishes, we cut up the chicken into fairly small pieces. Legs, for example, are always separated into drumsticks and thighs. Breasts are cut into 4–6 parts. Wings and backs are similarly cut up.

When one of my recipes calls for chicken parts, you can either buy a whole 3–3½ lb (1.5–1.75kg) chicken and cut it up yourself using a sharp knife and a cleaver or else you can buy chicken joints – the ones you prefer – and cut them up further, if necessary. I happen to have a family in which four members like dark meat and one only likes breast meat (unless it is a roast, when we all prefer breast meat). This does not make life easy. But I do have to keep everyone happy so I frequently resort to buying joints.

I have a few egg recipes in this chapter as well. If you are looking for a new, spicier approach to eggs, try *Ekoori*, scrambled eggs cooked with fresh green coriander and tomato or the pie-like *Parsi* omelette seasoned with cumin and green chillies. Indians also know how to convert plain, hard boiled eggs into the most delicious main courses by putting them into thick, creamy sauces or tart, vinegary ones.

Bombay-style chicken with red split lentils

Murghi aur masoor dal

This dish, in which chicken is combined with red lentils, is really like a hearty stew, just perfect for cold winter days. You could add vegetables to it as well, such as shelled peas or ½ inch (1cm) lengths of green beans. If you do this, put in the vegetables at about the same time as you put in the lemon juice.

Traditionally, rice is served on the side but, if you like, you could have this dish with thickly cut slices of some dark, crusty bread.

Serves 6–7:

9 oz (250g) red split lentils, picked over, washed, and drained

3 oz (75g) onion, peeled and chopped

½–1 fresh, hot green chilli, finely sliced

2 teaspoons ground cumin seeds

½ teaspoon ground turmeric

1 teaspoon very finely chopped, peeled ginger

2½ pints (1.5 litres) water

About 3 lb (1kg 350g) of jointed chicken parts, skinned

2¼ teaspoons salt

2 tablespoons vegetable oil

1 teaspoon whole cumin seeds

2–4 cloves garlic, peeled and finely chopped

¼–¾ teaspoon cayenne pepper

2 tablespoons lemon juice

½ teaspoon sugar

¼ teaspoon garam masala (see page 18)

Optional garnish: 3 tablespoons chopped fresh coriander

Combine the lentils, onion, green chilli, ground cumin, turmeric, half of the chopped ginger and 2½ pints (1.5 litres) water in a big, heavy pot. Bring to a simmer, cover, leaving the lid very slightly ajar, and cook on low heat for 45 minutes. Add the chicken and the salt. Mix and bring to a boil. Cover, turn heat to low and simmer gently for 25–30 minutes or until chicken is tender.

Heat the oil in a small frying pan over a medium flame. When hot, put in the whole cumin seeds. As soon as the seeds begin to sizzle – this just takes a few seconds – put in the remaining ½ teaspoon chopped ginger and garlic. Fry until the garlic turns slightly brown. Now put in the cayenne pepper. Lift up the frying pan immediately and pour its entire contents – oil and spices – into the pot with the chicken and lentils. Also add the lemon juice, sugar, and *garam masala*. Stir to mix and cook on a medium-low flame for another 5 minutes.

Sprinkle the fresh coriander over the top just before you serve.

Tandoori-style chicken

Tandoori murghi

I have, I think, found a way to make tandoori-style chicken without a tandoor! The tandoor, as I am sure you all know by now, is a vat-shaped clay oven, heated with charcoal or wood. The heat inside builds up to such an extent that small whole chickens, skewered and thrust into it, cook in about 10 minutes. This fierce heat seals the juices of the bird and keeps it moist while an earlier marinating process ensures that the chicken is tender and well flavoured. The result is quite spectacular.

To approximate a tandoor, I use an ordinary oven, pre-heated to its maximum temperature. Then, instead of cooking a whole bird, I use serving-sized pieces – legs that are cut into two and breasts that are quartered. The cooking time is not 10 minutes because home ovens do not get as hot as tandoors. Still, breasts cook in about 15–20 minutes and legs in 20–25 minutes.

Tandoori chicken may, of course, be served just the way it comes out of the oven with a few wedges of lemon, or it can, without much effort, be transformed into *Makkhani murghi* (see next recipe) by smothering it with a rich butter-cream-tomato sauce. Both dishes are excellent for dinner parties as most of the work can be done a day ahead of time. The chicken is marinated the night before so all you have to do on the day of the party is to cook it in the oven for a brief 20–25 minutes just before you sit down to eat. If you wish to make the sauce, all the ingredients for it except the butter may be combined in a bowl the day before and refrigerated. After that, the sauce cooks in less than five minutes and involves only one step – heating it. Both these chicken dishes may be served with rice or *naan* and a green bean or cauliflower dish.

OPPOSITE PAGE:
Spiced basmati rice, *Masaledar basmati* (page 148)
Aubergine cooked in the pickling style, *Baigan achari* (page 100)
Kashmiri red lamb stew, *Kashmiri rogan josh* (page 53)

OVERLEAF:
Cod steaks in a spicy tomato sauce, *Timatar wali macchi* (page 95)
Rice with peas, *Tahiri* (page 149)
Gujerati-style cabbage with carrots, *Sambhara* (page 106)

Serves 4–6:

2½ lb (1kg 125g) chicken pieces, skinned (you may use legs, breasts, or a combination of the two)

1 teaspoon salt

1 juicy lemon

15 fl oz (425ml) plain yoghurt

½ medium-sized onion, peeled and quartered

1 clove garlic, peeled

A ¾ inch (2cm) cube of fresh ginger, peeled and quartered

½ fresh, hot green chilli, roughly sliced

2 teaspoons garam masala (page 18)

3 tablespoons yellow liquid food colouring mixed with ½–1½ tablespoons red liquid food colouring, optional, see note below

Wedges of lime, optional

The traditional orange colour of cooked tandoori chicken comes from food colouring. You may or may not want to use it. If you do, mix yellow and red liquid food colours to get a bright orange shade. If your red is very dark, use only ½ tablespoon of it.

Cut each leg into two pieces and each breast into four pieces. Cut two long slits on each side of each part of the legs. The slits should never start at an edge and they should be deep enough to reach the bone. Cut similar slits on the meaty side of each breast piece.

Spread the chicken pieces out on one or two large platters. Sprinkle half the salt and squeeze the juice from three-quarters of a lemon over them. Lightly rub the salt and lemon juice into the slits. Turn the chicken pieces over and do the same on the other side with the remaining salt and lemon juice. Set aside for 20 minutes.

Combine the yoghurt, onion, garlic, ginger, green chilli and *garam masala* in the container of an electric blender or food processor. Blend until you have a smooth paste. Empty the paste into a strainer set over a large ceramic or stainless steel bowl. Push the paste through.

Brush the chicken pieces on both sides with the food colouring and then put them with any accumulated juices and any remaining food colouring into the bowl with the marinade. Mix well, making sure that the marinade goes into the slits in the chicken. Cover and refrigerate for 6–24 hours (the longer the better).

Preheat the oven to its maximum temperature.

Take the chicken pieces out of the bowl, shaking off as much of the marinade as possible. Arrange them in a large shallow baking tray in a single layer. Bake for 20–25 minutes or until just done. You might test the chicken with a fork just to be sure. Serve hot, with lime wedges.

N.B. The left over marinade may be frozen, and re-used *once*.

Chicken in a butter sauce

Makkhani murghi

The sauce in this dish should be folded into butter at the very last minute as it tends to separate otherwise. However, you can combine all the ingredients except the butter up to a day ahead of time and refrigerate them until they are needed.

This is a wonderfully simple but spectacular dish in which the Tandoori chicken of the preceding recipe is transformed with a sauce.

Serves 4–6:

4 tablespoons tomato purée

Water to mix

A 1 inch (2.5cm) cube of fresh ginger, peeled and grated very finely to a pulp

$\frac{1}{2}$ pint (275ml) single cream

1 teaspoon garam masala (page 18)

$\frac{3}{4}$ teaspoon salt

$\frac{1}{4}$ teaspoon sugar

1 fresh, hot green chilli, finely chopped

$\frac{1}{4}$ teaspoon cayenne pepper

1 tablespoon very finely chopped fresh green coriander

4 teaspoons lemon juice

1 teaspoon ground roasted cumin seeds (see page 17)

4 oz (110g) unsalted butter

Tandoori-style chicken, freshly cooked according to the preceding recipe

Put the tomato paste in a clear measuring jug. Add water slowly, mixing as you go, to make up 8 fl oz (225ml) of tomato sauce. Add the ginger, cream, *garam masala*, salt, sugar, green chilli, cayenne, green coriander, lemon juice, and ground roasted cumin seeds. Mix well.

Heat the butter in a wide sauté pan or a large frying pan. When the butter has melted, add all the ingredients in the measuring jug. Bring to a simmer and cook on medium heat for a minute, mixing in the butter as you do so. Add the chicken pieces (but not their accumulated juices). Stir once and put chicken pieces on a warm serving platter. Extra sauce should be spooned over the top.

NB, cashew nuts – Pulse = v. fine add to melted Butter. add back to sauce

Spicy baked chicken

Masaledar murghi

Here is one of those easy chicken dishes that can be prepared almost effortlessly. There is a marinating period, though, of about 3 hours.

This chicken has a very red look which it gets from ground, hot red chillies. To get the same effect – and not all of the heat – you can combine paprika with cayenne pepper in any proportion that you like as long as the total quantity is about $1\frac{1}{2}$ tablespoons.

I like to serve this chicken with 'Rice with peas' (page 149) and 'Red split lentils' (page 122).

Serves 6:

1 tablespoon ground cumin seeds

1 tablespoon paprika

$1\frac{1}{2}$ teaspoons cayenne pepper (see note above)

1 tablespoon ground turmeric

$1-1\frac{1}{2}$ teaspoons freshly ground black pepper

$2\frac{1}{2}-3$ teaspoons salt – or to taste

2–3 cloves garlic, peeled and mashed to a pulp

6 tablespoons lemon juice

$3\frac{1}{2}$ lb (1kg 500g) chicken pieces

3 tablespoons vegetable oil

Combine the cumin, paprika, cayenne, turmeric, black pepper, salt, garlic, and lemon juice in a bowl. Mix well. Rub this mixture over the chicken pieces, pushing the paste inside any flaps and openings that you can find. Stuff some paste along the bone of the drumsticks. Spread the chicken pieces in a shallow baking tray, skin side down, and set aside in a cool place for 3 hours. (Longer will not hurt. Just cover the chicken with cling film to prevent it from drying out.)

Preheat the oven to gas mark 6, 400°F (200°C). Brush the tops of the chicken pieces with the oil. Put the chicken in the oven and bake for 20 minutes. Turn the chicken pieces over and bake another 25 minutes or until chicken is tender. Baste the chicken pieces with the drippings 3–4 times. If a lot of liquid accumulates in your baking tray, remove the extra fat with a spoon. Then pour the remaining liquid into a small pot. Boil down until the sauce is somewhat reduced. Arrange the chicken pieces on a platter, pour the reduced sauce over them and serve at once.

Chicken in a fried onion sauce

Murghi rasedar

This is how I cook the dish that my children refer to as our 'everyday' chicken. We tend to eat it with plain basmati rice and 'Carrot and onion salad' (page 171).

Serves 4–6:

2½ lb (1kg 125g) chicken joints

12 oz (350g) onions, peeled

A 1½ inch (4cm) cube of fresh ginger, peeled and coarsely chopped

6 cloves garlic, peeled

7 tablespoons vegetable oil

1 tablespoon ground coriander seeds

1 tablespoon ground cumin seeds

½ teaspoon ground turmeric

¼–½ teaspoon cayenne pepper

4 tablespoons plain yoghurt

1 pint (570ml) water

8 oz (225g) tomatoes, peeled (see page 29) and very finely chopped (tinned tomatoes may be substituted)

2 teaspoons salt

½ teaspoon garam masala (page 18)

1 tablespoon finely chopped fresh green coriander (parsley may be substituted)

Cut the chicken into serving pieces. Whole legs should be separated into drumsticks and thighs. Whole breasts should be cut into 4–6 pieces, depending on their size. Skin all the chicken pieces.

Chop half of the onions coarsely. Cut the remaining onions into halves, lengthwise, and then crosswise into very thin slices.

Put the chopped onions, ginger, and garlic into the container of a food processor or blender. Blend until you have a paste.

Heat the oil in a large, wide pot or a large, deep frying pan (preferably non-stick) over a medium flame. When hot, put in the sliced onions. Stir and fry the onions until they are a deep, reddish-brown colour. Remove the onions with a slotted spoon, squeezing out and leaving behind as much of the oil as possible. Put the onions in a plate and set aside.

Take the pot off the flame. Put in the blended paste (keep face averted). Put the pot back on the heat. Stir and fry the paste until it is brown, about 3–4 minutes. Now put in the coriander, cumin, turmeric and cayenne, stir once. Put in 1 tablespoon of the yoghurt. Stir for about 30 seconds or until it has been incorporated into the sauce. Add all the yoghurt this way, one tablespoon at a time. Put in the chicken pieces and stir them around for a minute.

Pour in the water, add the tomatoes and salt. Stir to mix and bring to a simmer. Cover, turn heat to low and cook for 20 minutes. Sprinkle in the *garam masala* and the fried onions. Mix. Cook, uncovered, on medium heat for 7–8 minutes or until the sauce reduces and thickens.

Skim off the fat and put the chicken in a warm serving dish. Sprinkle the green coriander over the top.

Lemony chicken with fresh coriander

Hare masale wali murghi

Here is a delightful lemony, gingery dish that requires quite a lot of fresh coriander. It is a great favourite with our family. I generally serve it with 'Spiced basmati rice' (page 148).

Serves 6:

Two 1 inch (2.5cm) cubes of fresh ginger, peeled and coarsely chopped

4 tablespoons plus 5 fl oz (150ml) water

6 tablespoons vegetable oil

2½ lb (1kg 175g) chicken parts, skinned

5 cloves garlic, peeled and very finely chopped

7 oz (200g) fresh coriander (weight without roots and lower stems) very finely chopped

½–1 fresh, hot green chilli, very finely chopped

¼ teaspoon cayenne pepper

2 teaspoons ground cumin seeds

1 teaspoon ground coriander seeds

½ teaspoon ground turmeric

1 teaspoon salt – or to taste

2 tablespoons lemon juice

Put the ginger and 4 tablespoons of the water into the container of an electric blender. Blend until you have a paste.

Heat the oil in a wide, heavy, preferably non-stick pot over a medium-high flame. When hot, put in as many chicken pieces as the pot will hold in a single layer and brown on both sides. Remove the chicken pieces with a slotted spoon and put them in a bowl. Brown all the chicken pieces this way.

Put the garlic into the same hot oil. As soon as the pieces turn a medium brown colour, turn heat to medium and pour in the paste from the blender. Stir and fry it for a minute. Now add the fresh coriander, green chilli, cayenne, ground cumin, ground coriander seeds, turmeric, and salt. Stir and cook for a minute. Put in all the chicken pieces as well as any liquid that might have accumulated in the chicken bowl. Also add 5 fl oz (150ml) water and the lemon juice. Stir and bring to a boil. Cover tightly, turn heat to low and cook for 15 minutes. Turn the chicken pieces over. Cover again and cook another 10–15 minutes or until chicken is tender. If the sauce is too thin, uncover the pot and boil some of it away over a slightly higher heat.

Chicken with cream

Malai wali murghi

This rich, creamy dish may be served with 'Aubergine cooked in the pickling style' (page 100) and rice.

Serves 6:

3 lb (1kg 350g) of jointed chicken parts, skinned

1½ teaspoons salt

2 teaspoons ground cumin seeds

1½ teaspoons ground coriander seeds

½ teaspoon ground turmeric

½ teaspoon cayenne pepper

Freshly ground black pepper

6–7 cloves of garlic, peeled

A 1 inch (2.5cm) cube of fresh ginger, peeled and coarsely chopped

11 fl oz (300ml) water

6 tablespoons vegetable oil

4 oz (110g) onion, peeled and finely chopped

6 oz (175g) tomato, peeled (see page 29) and finely chopped

4 tablespoons plain yoghurt

1 teaspoon garam masala (page 18)

6 tablespoons double cream

Sprinkle ½ teaspoon of the salt, 1 teaspoon ground cumin, ½ teaspoon ground coriander, ¼ teaspoon ground turmeric, ¼ teaspoon cayenne and some black pepper on the chicken parts. Mix well and set aside for at least one hour.

Put the garlic and ginger into the container of an electric blender or food processor. Add 4 fl oz (125ml) of the water and blend until fairly smooth.

Heat the oil in a wide, preferably non-stick pot over a medium-high flame. When hot, put in as many chicken pieces as the pot will hold easily in a single layer and brown lightly on both sides. Remove with a slotted spoon and set aside in a bowl. Brown all the chicken pieces the same way.

Put the chopped onion into the remaining oil. Stir and fry until the pieces turn a medium-brown colour. Add the garlic-ginger paste. Stir and fry until all the water from the paste evaporates and you see the oil again. Put in the remaining 1 teaspoon cumin, 1 teaspoon coriander, ¼ teaspoon turmeric, and ¼ teaspoon cayenne. Stir and fry for about 20 seconds. Now put in the chopped tomato. Turn the heat down to a medium-low. Stir and cook the spice paste for 3–4 minutes, mashing the tomato pieces with the back of a slotted spoon as you do so. Add the yoghurt, a tablespoon at a time, incorporating it into the sauce each time before you add any more. Put in the chicken pieces and any accumulated juices, the remaining 7 fl oz (300ml) water and 1 teaspoon salt. Bring to a boil. Cover, turn heat to low and simmer for 20 minutes. Take off the cover. Add the *garam masala* and cream. Mix gently. Turn the heat up to medium-high and cook, stirring gently now and then, until the sauce has reduced somewhat and turned fairly thick.

Chicken with tomatoes and *garam masala*
Timatar murghi

This simple chicken dish is a great favourite with our children. I generally serve it with plain long-grain rice and 'Whole green lentils with garlic and onion' (page 124).

Serves 6:

5 tablespoons vegetable oil

$\frac{3}{4}$ teaspoon whole cumin seeds

A 1 inch (2.5cm) stick of cinnamon

6 whole cardamom pods

2 bay leaves

$\frac{1}{4}$ teaspoon whole peppercorns

6 oz (175g) onions, peeled and finely chopped

6–7 cloves garlic, peeled and finely chopped

A 1 inch (2.5cm) cube of fresh ginger, peeled and finely chopped

1 lb (450g) fresh tomatoes, peeled (see page 29) and finely chopped (tinned tomatoes may be substituted)

3 lb (1kg 350g) jointed chicken pieces, skinned

$1\frac{1}{2}$ teaspoons salt

$\frac{1}{8}$–$\frac{1}{2}$ teaspoon cayenne pepper

$\frac{1}{2}$ teaspoon garam masala (page 18)

Heat the oil in a large, wide pot over a medium-high flame. When hot, put in the cumin seeds, cinnamon, cardamom, bay leaves, and peppercorns. Stir once and then put in the onions, garlic, and ginger. Stir this mixture around until the onion picks up brown specks. Now put in the tomatoes, chicken, salt, and cayenne pepper. Stir to mix and bring to a boil. Cover tightly, turn heat to low and simmer for 25 minutes or until chicken is tender. Stir a few times during this cooking period. Remove cover and turn up heat to medium. Sprinkle in the *garam masala* and cook, stirring gently for about 5 minutes in order to reduce the liquid somewhat.

N.B. The whole spices in this dish should not be eaten.

Mughlai chicken with almonds and sultanas

Shahjahani murghi

This elegant, mild dish is very suitable for dinner parties. It could be accompanied by 'Spiced basmati rice' (page 148), 'Cauliflower with potatoes' (page 109), and 'Yoghurt with walnuts and fresh coriander' (page 163).

Serves 6:

A 1 inch (2.5cm) cube of fresh ginger, peeled and coarsely chopped

8–9 cloves garlic, peeled

6 tablespoons blanched, slivered almonds

4 tablespoons of water

7 tablespoons vegetable oil

3 lb (1kg 350g) chicken pieces, skinned

10 whole cardamom pods

A 1 inch (2.5cm) stick of cinnamon

2 bay leaves

5 whole cloves

7 oz (200g) onions, peeled and finely chopped

2 teaspoons ground cumin seeds

$\frac{1}{8}$–$\frac{1}{2}$ teaspoon cayenne pepper

7 tablespoons plain yoghurt

1$\frac{1}{2}$ teaspoons salt

$\frac{1}{2}$ pint (275ml) single cream

1–2 tablespoons sultanas

$\frac{1}{4}$ teaspoon garam masala (page 18)

Put the ginger, garlic, 4 tablespoons of the almonds, and 4 tablespoons water into the container of an electric blender and blend until you have a paste.

Heat the oil in a wide, preferably non-stick pot or deep frying pan over a medium–high flame. When hot, put in as many chicken pieces as the pot will hold in a single layer. Let the chicken pieces turn golden brown on the bottom. Now turn all the pieces over and brown the second side. Remove the chicken pieces with a slotted spoon and put them in a bowl. Brown all the chicken pieces this way.

Put the cardamom, cinnamon, bay leaves, and cloves into the same hot oil. Stir and fry them for a few seconds. Now put in the onions. Stir and fry the onions for 3–4 minutes or until they are lightly browned. Put in the paste from the blender, the cumin, and cayenne. Stir and fry for 2–3 minutes or until the oil seems to separate from the spice mixture and the spices are lightly browned. Add 1 tablespoon of the yoghurt. Stir and fry it for about 30 seconds. Now add another tablespoon of yoghurt. Keep doing this until all the yoghurt has been incorporated.

Put in the chicken pieces, any liquid that might have accumulated in the chicken bowl, the cream, and salt. Bring to a simmer. Cover, turn heat to low and cook gently for 20 minutes. Add the sultanas and turn over the chicken pieces. Cover and cook another 10 minutes or until the chicken is tender. Add the *garam masala*. Stir to mix.

Put the remaining almonds in a baking tray and put them under the grill until they brown lightly. You will have to toss them frequently. Sprinkle these almonds over the chicken when you serve.

(Extra fat may be spooned off the top just before serving. The whole spices in the dish are not meant to be eaten.)

Goan-style chicken with roasted coconut

Shakoothi

I just love this dish. I ate it for the first time in balmy, palm-fringed, coastal Goa, and have been hoarding the recipe ever since. Even though there are several steps to the recipe, it is not at all hard to put together, especially if you have grated coconut sitting around in the freezer, as I always have. I am now in the habit of buying two or three coconuts whenever I see any good ones. I grate them as soon as I get home (for instructions, see page 15) and then store the grated flesh in flattened plastic packets. Defrosting takes no time at all. This way, I am always ready, not only to make *shakoothi*, but to sprinkle fresh coconut over meats and vegetables whenever I want to.

You could serve this dish with plain long-grain rice, 'Spicy green beans' (page 103) and 'Onion relish' (page 174).

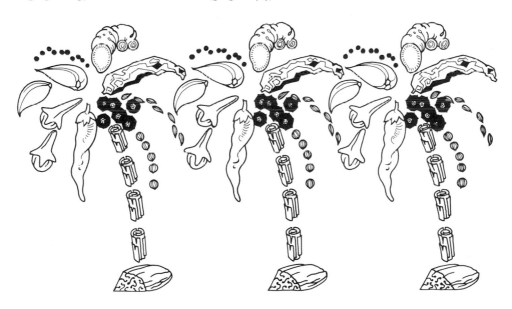

Serves 4–5:

1½ tablespoons whole coriander seeds
1½ teaspoons whole cumin seeds
1 teaspoon whole black mustard seeds
A 1 inch (2.5cm) stick of cinnamon, broken up into 3–4 pieces
4 whole cloves
¼ teaspoon whole black peppercorns
About ⅙ of a whole nutmeg
1 whole, dried hot red chilli (remove seeds if you want it mild)
Enough grated fresh coconut (see page 15) to fill a glass measuring jug to the 15 fl oz (425ml) level
6–8 cloves garlic, peeled
A 1 inch (2.5cm) cube of fresh ginger, peeled and coarsely chopped
½–1 fresh, hot green chilli
4 tablespoons plus ½ pint (275ml) water
4 tablespoons vegetable oil
6 oz (175g) onions, peeled and minced
2¼ lb (1kg) jointed chicken parts, skinned
1½ teaspoons salt

Put the coriander seeds, cumin seeds, mustard seeds, cinnamon, cloves, peppercorns, nutmeg and red chilli in a small, preferably cast-iron frying pan. Place the pan over a medium flame. Now quickly 'dry-roast' the spices, stirring them frequently until they emit a very pleasant 'roasted' aroma. Empty the spices into a clean coffee grinder or spice grinder and grind until fine. Take the spices out and put them in a bowl.

Put the coconut into the same frying pan and dry-roast it over a medium flame, stirring it all the time. The coconut should pick up lots of brown flecks and also smell 'roasted'. Put the coconut in the bowl with the other dry roasted spices.

Put the garlic, ginger, and green chilli into the container of an electric blender, along with 4 tablespoons water. Blend until you have a paste.

Heat the oil in a 10–12 inch (25–30cm) frying pan or sauté pan over a medium-high flame. When hot, put in the onions. Stir and fry them until they pick up brown spots. Now pour in the garlic-ginger mixture from the blender and stir once. Turn heat to medium. Put in the chicken pieces, salt, as well as the spice-coconut mixture in the bowl. Stir and fry the chicken for 3–4 minutes or until it loses its pinkness and turns slightly brown. Add ½ pint (275ml) water and bring to a simmer. Cover tightly, turn heat to low, and cook for 25–30 minutes or until chicken is tender. Stir a few times during this cooking period, making sure that you turn over each piece of chicken so that it gets evenly coloured.

Chicken in a red sweet pepper sauce

Lal masale wali murghi

Many of the meat, poultry, and fish dishes which are traditional along India's west coast have thick and stunningly red-looking sauces. The main ingredient, which provides both the texture and the colour, are red chillies – either fresh, or dried. It is almost impossible to find the correct variety of red chilli in Britain – one that is bright red and just mildly hot. What I have discovered, though, is that a combination of red peppers and cayenne pepper works exceedingly well!

I like to serve this dish with 'Aromatic yellow rice' (page 153), and 'Yoghurt with aubergine' (page 164).

Serves 4:

2¼ lb (1kg) chicken parts (either drumsticks and thighs and/or breast)
4 oz (110g) onions, peeled and coarsely chopped
A 1 inch (2.5cm) cube of fresh ginger, peeled and coarsely chopped
3 cloves garlic, peeled
1 oz (25g) blanched, slivered almonds
¾ lb (350g) red sweet-peppers trimmed, seeded, and coarsely chopped
1 tablespoon ground cumin seeds
2 teaspoons ground coriander seeds
½ teaspoon ground turmeric
⅛–½ teaspoon cayenne pepper
2 teaspoon salt
7 tablespoons vegetable oil
8 fl oz (225ml) water
2 tablespoons lemon juice
½ teaspoon coarsely ground black pepper

If chicken legs are whole, divide drumsticks from thighs with a sharp knife. Breasts should be cut into four parts. Skin all chicken pieces.

Combine onions, ginger, garlic, almonds, peppers, cumin, coriander, turmeric, cayenne, and salt in the container of a food processor or blender. Blend, pushing down with a rubber spatula whenever you need to, until you have a paste.

Put the oil in a large, wide, and preferably non-stick pan and heat it over a medium-high flame. When hot, pour in all the paste from the food processor or blender. Stir and fry the paste for 10–12 minutes or until you can see the oil forming tiny bubbles around it.

Put in the chicken, with the 8 fl oz (225ml) water, lemon juice, and black pepper. Stir to mix and bring to a boil. Cover, turn heat to low and simmer gently for 25 minutes or until the chicken is tender. Stir a few times during this cooking period.

Whole chicken, baked in aluminium foil

Murgh musallam

Over the years, as I am more and more rushed for time, I find myself simplifying some of my own recipes. The traditional *murgh musallam* recipe, for example, is quite a complicated one. I now cook it relatively simply, by smothering a marinaded bird with a spice paste, wrapping it in foil and popping it into the oven. It works beautifully.

I like to serve this dish with 'Mushroom pullao' (page 152), 'Spinach cooked with onions' (page 115) and 'Yoghurt with cucumber and mint' (page 162).

Serves 4–6:

For the marinade:

A 1 inch (2.5cm) cube of fresh ginger, peeled and coarsely chopped

2 large cloves garlic, peeled

6 tablespoons plain yoghurt

½ teaspoon ground turmeric

1¼ teaspoons salt

¼–½ teaspoon cayenne pepper

Freshly ground black pepper

Make the marinade: Put the ginger, garlic, and 3 tablespoons of the yoghurt into the container of a food processor or blender. Blend, pushing down with a rubber spatula whenever you need to, until you have a paste. Add the turmeric, salt, cayenne, and black pepper. Blend for a second to mix. Empty the marinade into a bowl. (Do not wash out the food processor or blender yet.) Add the remaining 3 tablespoons of the yoghurt to the marinade and beat it in with a fork.

Skin the entire chicken with the exception of the wing tips. Skin the neck. Put the chicken, breast up, in a platter and put the giblets somewhere near it. Rub the chicken, inside and out, as well as the giblets, with the marinade. Set aside, unrefrigerated, for 2 hours.

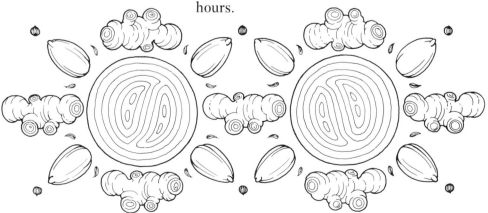

You also need:

A whole, $3\frac{1}{2}$ lb (1kg 500g) chicken

8 oz (225g) onions

4 cloves garlic, peeled

A $1\frac{1}{2}$ inch (4cm) cube of fresh ginger, peeled and coarsely chopped

1 oz (25g) blanched, slivered almonds

2 teaspoons ground cumin seeds

2 teaspoons ground coriander seeds

$\frac{1}{2}$ teaspoon ground turmeric

1 tablespoon ground paprika

$\frac{1}{4}$ teaspoon cayenne pepper

$1\frac{1}{2}$ teaspoons salt

8 tablespoons vegetable oil

2 tablespoons lemon juice

$\frac{1}{2}$ teaspoon coarsely ground black pepper

$\frac{1}{2}$ teaspoon garam masala (see page 18)

Meanwhile, put the onions, garlic, ginger, and almonds into the food processor or blender. Blend, pushing down with a rubber spatula whenever you need to, until you have a paste. Add the cumin, coriander, turmeric, paprika, cayenne, and salt. Blend again to mix.

Heat the oil in a large, non-stick pan over a medium-high flame. Put in the paste from the food processor or blender. Fry, stirring, for 8–9 minutes. Add the lemon juice, black pepper, and *garam masala*. Mix. Turn off the heat and let the paste cool.

Preheat oven to gas mark 4, 350°F (180°C).

When the chicken has finished sitting in its marinade for 2 hours, spread out a piece of aluminium foil, large enough to enclose the chicken. Put the chicken, breast up, in the centre of the foil and put the giblets somewhere near it. Rub the chicken, inside and out, as well as the giblets, with the fried spice paste. Bring the ends of the foil towards the centre to form a tight packet. All 'seams' should be 2 inches (5cm) above the 'floor' of the packet. Put the wrapped chicken, breast up, on a baking tray and bake in a pre-heated oven for $1\frac{1}{2}$ hours or until tender.

Vegetable omelette

Parsi omlate

The Parsis who settled on India's west coast around the Bombay area, came originally from Persia over a thousand years ago. Even though they have proudly retained their religion, Zoroastrianism, they have been unafraid to let their adopted country or, for that matter, British colonialists, influence them in their choice of dress, language, and food. The Parsi culinary tradition is unique, borrowing freely as it does from Gujeratis, Maharashtrians, and the English. But there is a Persian streak in there as well. This can best be seen in the fondness for eggs and the abundance of egg dishes – eggs over fried okra, eggs over matchstick potatoes, eggs over tomato chutney – the list is long. Parsis also make all kinds of omelettes. Some are folded in the traditional way but many others are round and pie-like. The recipe here is for a pie-like omelette, filled with vegetables.

This omelette has become one of my favourite brunch dishes now. It may be served, Western-style, with a salad, French bread and white wine, or it may be served Indian-style, with a stack of *parathas* or toast, 'Tomato, onion and green coriander relish' (page 172), and steaming hot tea.

To make this omelette properly, it really helps to have a non-stick frying pan. The one I use measures $7\frac{1}{2}$ inches (19cm) across at the bottom, curving up to 10 inches (25cm) across at the top. It is 2 inches (5cm) in height. Your pan may have a somewhat different shape. It does not really matter. Just remember that the pie-shaped omelette rises slightly as it is cooking so a little space has to be left at the top. You also need a lid. If your frying pan does not have one, use aluminium foil.

Serves 4–6:

1 lb (450g) courgettes

$1\frac{3}{4}$ teaspoons salt – or to taste

5 tablespoons vegetable oil

4 oz (110g) onions, peeled and finely chopped

5 oz (150g) potatoes, peeled and cut into $\frac{1}{4}$ inch (5mm) dice

1–3 fresh, hot green chillies, finely chopped

7 oz (200g) tomatoes, chopped

$1\frac{1}{2}$ teaspoons ground cumin seeds

$\frac{1}{8}$–$\frac{1}{4}$ teaspoon cayenne pepper, optional

Freshly ground black pepper

9 large eggs

3 tablespoons finely chopped fresh green coriander (use parsley as a substitute)

$\frac{1}{4}$ teaspoon baking soda

Trim and discard the ends of the courgettes and then grate them coarsely. Put the grated courgettes in a bowl. Sprinkle $\frac{3}{4}$ teaspoon salt over them and mix thoroughly. Set aside for 30 minutes. Squeeze all the liquid out of the grated courgettes and then separate the strands so they are no longer bunched up.

Heat 3 tablespoons oil in a non-stick frying pan (see note at the top of the recipe) over a medium flame. When hot, put in the onions. Stir and fry for a minute. Now put in the potatoes and the green chillies. Stir and fry for about 5 minutes or until the potato pieces are just about tender. Add the courgettes, tomatoes, cumin, the remaining 1 teaspoon salt, cayenne, and a generous amount of black pepper. Stir and cook for 2–3 minutes or until the tomato pieces are soft. Set aside to cool.

Break the eggs into a bowl and beat well. Empty the cooled vegetable mixture into the beaten eggs and add the fresh green coriander. Stir to mix. Sprinkle in the baking soda, making sure that it is lump-free. Mix again.

Wipe out the frying pan with a piece of kitchen paper. Pour in the remaining 2 tablespoons of oil and set to heat on a low flame. When hot, pour in the egg mixture.

Cover and cook on low heat for 15 minutes. Remove the cover. Now you have to turn the omelette over. Do it this way: Invert a large plate over the frying pan. Place one hand on the plate. Quickly and deftly, lift the frying pan up with the other hand and turn it upside down over the plate. Your omelette will now be in the plate with its browned side on top. Slip it back into the frying pan and cook it, uncovered, for 5 minutes. Invert the omelette once again on to a serving platter. The lighter side should now be on the top.

Serve hot, warm, or at room temperature.

Spicy scrambled eggs

Ekoori

Ekoori is the Parsi name for them but scrambled eggs, cooked in a similar style, are eaten all over India. Eat them with toast or any Indian bread.

Serves 4:
3 tablespoons unsalted butter or vegetable oil
1 small onion, peeled and finely chopped
½ teaspoon peeled and very finely grated fresh ginger
½–1 fresh, hot green chilli, finely chopped
1 tablespoon very finely chopped fresh green coriander
⅛ teaspoon ground turmeric
½ teaspoon ground cumin seeds
1 small tomato, peeled (see page 29) and chopped
6 large eggs, lightly beaten
Salt and freshly ground pepper to taste

Melt the butter in a medium sized, preferably non-stick frying pan over medium heat. Put in the onion and sauté until soft. Add the ginger, chilli, fresh green coriander, turmeric, cumin and tomato. Stir and cook for 3–4 minutes or until tomatoes are soft.

Put in the beaten eggs. Salt and pepper them lightly. Stir the eggs gently until they form soft, thick curds. Cook the scrambled eggs to any consistency you like.

Hard boiled eggs in a spicy cream sauce
Malaidar unday

This delicious egg dish can be put together rather quickly and is just perfect for brunches, light lunches, and suppers. You could serve toast on the side or, if you like, rice and a crisp salad. If you prefer to serve a more traditional Indian meal, then *parathas* or spiced basmati rice and 'Gujerati-style green beans' (page 102) would be suitable accompaniments.

This recipe calls for a small amount of chicken stock. If you have some home-made stock handy, well and good. Otherwise, use stock made with a cube, but adjust your salt as cube stock can be salty.

Serves 3–4:

3 tablespoons vegetable oil

2 oz (50g) onion, peeled and finely chopped

A 1 inch (2.5cm) cube of fresh ginger, peeled and finely grated

½–1 fresh, hot green chilli, finely chopped

½ pint (275ml) single cream

1 tablespoon lemon juice

1 teaspoon ground, roasted cumin seeds (see page 17)

⅛ teaspoon cayenne pepper

½ teaspoon salt

¼ teaspoon garam masala (see page 18)

2 teaspoons tomato paste

¼ pint (150ml) chicken stock

6–8 hard boiled eggs, peeled and cut crosswise into halves

1 tablespoon finely chopped fresh green coriander or parsley, optional

Heat the oil over medium heat in a large, preferably non-stick frying pan. When hot, put in the onions. Stir and fry the onions for about 3 minutes or until the pieces are browned at the edges. Put in the ginger and chilli. Stir and fry for a minute. Now put in the cream, lemon juice, ground roasted cumin, cayenne, salt, *garam masala*, tomato paste, and chicken stock. Stir to mix thoroughly and bring to a simmer.

Put all the egg halves into the sauce in a single layer, cut side up. Spoon the sauce over them. Cook over medium heat for about 5 minutes, spooning the sauce frequently over the eggs as you do so. By this time the sauce will have become fairly thick. Put the egg halves carefully in a serving dish, cut side up, and pour the sauce over them. Garnish with the fresh green coriander, sprinkling it lightly over the top.

Vinegared eggs

Baida vindaloo

This vinegary, hard-boiled egg dish is almost like a pickle and perfect for taking out on picnics. It is, like all Goan-style *vindaloo* dishes, tart, hot, garlicky and just very slightly sweet. I have lessened the tartness somewhat by cooking the eggs in a mixture of vinegar and water instead of just vinegar. Use the mildest vinegar that you can find. In this recipe, you may use anywhere from 6 to 8 eggs without having to alter any of the other ingredients.

You could serve this dish with rice or an Indian bread. 'Cauliflower and potatoes' (page 109) would make a nice accompaniment.

Serves 3–4:
4 cloves garlic, peeled
A 1 inch (2.5cm) cube of fresh ginger, peeled and very finely grated
$\frac{1}{8}$–$\frac{1}{2}$ teaspoon cayenne pepper
2 teaspoons paprika
1$\frac{1}{2}$ teaspoons ground cumin seeds
1$\frac{1}{4}$ teaspoons salt
1$\frac{1}{2}$ tablespoons brown sugar
2 tablespoons plus 4 fl oz (150ml) mild white vinegar
3 tablespoons vegetable oil
A 1 inch (2.5cm) stick of cinnamon
$\frac{1}{2}$ lb (225g) onions, peeled and finely chopped
6 fl oz (175ml) water
$\frac{1}{2}$ teaspoon garam masala (page 18)
6–8 hard-boiled eggs, peeled and cut crosswise into halves

Mash the garlic cloves to a pulp or put them through a garlic press.

Combine the garlic, ginger, cayenne, paprika, cumin, salt, brown sugar and 2 tablespoons of vinegar in a cup or small bowl. Mix well.

Heat the oil in a medium-sized frying pan over medium heat. When hot, put in the cinnamon stick. Let it sizzle for a few seconds. Now put in all the onions. Stir and fry for about 5 minutes or until the onions have softened. Put in the paste from the cup as well as the *garam masala*. Stir and fry for 2 minutes. Add the 4 fl oz (150ml) vinegar as well as 6 fl oz (175ml) water. Stir to mix and bring to a simmer. Put all the egg halves into the frying pan in a single layer, cut side up and spoon the sauce over them. Cook on medium heat for about 5 minutes or until the sauce has thickened. Spoon the sauce frequently over the eggs as you do so.

Hard boiled eggs cooked with potatoes

Unday aur aloo

This simple dish is quite a family favourite. We eat it with an Indian bread or plain rice. It makes a pleasant change from meat, and is economical too.

Serves 2–4:

2 cloves garlic, peeled

A 1 inch (2.5cm) cube of fresh ginger, peeled and coarsely chopped

2 tablespoons plus ½ pint (275ml) water

1 lb (450g) potatoes, peeled

6 tablespoons vegetable oil

5 oz (150g) onions, peeled and finely chopped

⅛ teaspoon cayenne pepper

1 tablespoon ground coriander seeds

1 teaspoon plain flour

4 tablespoons plain yoghurt

11 oz (300g) tomatoes, peeled (see page 29) and finely chopped

1½ teaspoons salt

½ teaspoon garam masala (page 18)

1 tablespoon very finely chopped fresh green coriander (parsley may be substituted)

4 hard-boiled eggs, peeled

Put the garlic, ginger, and 2 tablespoons water into the container of a food processor or blender and blend until you have a paste.

Cut the potatoes into ½ inch (1cm) thick slices. Now cut the slices lengthwise into ½ inch (1cm) wide chips.

Heat the oil in a large, preferably non-stick frying pan over a medium-high flame. When hot, put in the potatoes. Turn and fry them until all sides turn golden brown. The potatoes should not cook through. Remove them with a slotted spoon and put aside on a plate.

Put the onions into the same oil. Stir and fry until they turn medium brown. Now put in the garlic-ginger paste. Stir and fry for a minute. Put in the cayenne, coriander and flour. Sir for a minute. Put in 1 tablespoon of the yoghurt. Stir for about 30 seconds or until it has been incorporated into the sauce. Add all the yoghurt this way, one tablespoon at a time. Now put in the tomatoes. Stir and fry for 2 minutes. Add ½ pint (275ml) water and the salt. Bring to a boil. Cover the frying pan, turn heat to low and simmer for 10 minutes.

Put the potatoes into the sauce and bring to a simmer. Cover, turn heat to low and simmer for 10 minutes or until potatoes are just tender. Add the *garam masala* and the green coriander. Stir gently to mix.

Halve the eggs, crosswise, and carefully put them into the frying pan with the cut sides up. Try not to let the yolk fall out. Spoon some sauce over the eggs. Bring to a simmer. Cover and simmer on low heat for 5 minutes.

FISH

There is nothing quite like good fresh fish. It is light, cooks fast, and may be prepared simply and elegantly at the same time. Needless to say, the types of fish available in Indian rivers, lakes, and seas are different from the ones found in the colder British waters. What used to be one of the common seafoods, fresh uncooked prawns, seems to have disappeared entirely from markets in Britain. I am hard put to understand why, since they can be found all over France, just a few miles away.

What I have done for this chapter is to work out Indian-style recipes for the fish that are commonly available in Britain. The prawns I have used are the cooked, packed frozen ones that are found in supermarkets, or freezer centres and fishmongers. Just look for the largest and best varieties that you can find.

Indians eat a fair amount of breaded, fried fish. I have used plaice for this as it is similar to our pomfret, at least in general shape. Our mackerel has a plumper form but is very similar in taste. So I have used it for a west coast recipe that calls for a fresh coriander and lemon marinade. We have no cod, halibut or haddock in India but the textures of some of our river fish are similar. I have used them in Indian-style recipes in which they are cooked with tomatoes or yoghurt or cauliflower.

I have even included a recipe for mussels. This is a Goan recipe, one of the few in this book that uses fresh coconut. It is an exquisite dish that can be made either with cockles or mussels.

I need hardly repeat that if you are buying fresh fish, make sure that it *is* fresh. The gills should be bright red, the eyes clear, the skin shiny, and the body firm and taut. The fish should not have a pronounced fishy odour.

Goan-style mussels

Thisra

Although eaten with rice in Goa, I love to serve these mussels all by themselves as a first course.

Serves 6:

30–36 small to medium-sized mussels

A 1 inch (2.5cm) cube of fresh ginger, peeled and coarsely chopped

8 cloves of garlic, peeled

12 fl oz (350ml) water

4 tablespoons vegetable oil

6–7 oz (175–200g) onions, peeled and chopped

1½–2 fresh, hot green chillies, sliced into fine rounds

½ teaspoon ground turmeric

2 teaspoons ground cumin seeds

Half of a fresh coconut, fincly grated (page 15)

½ teaspoon salt

Wash and scrub the mussels well, removing the beards that are often attached to them. Discard any shells that are open.

Put the ginger and garlic into the container of an electric blender or food processor. Add 4 fl oz (110ml) water and blend until fairly smooth.

Heat the oil in a large pot over a medium flame. When hot, put in the onions and sauté them until they turn translucent. Now put in the paste from the blender, green chillies, turmeric and cumin. Stir and fry for a minute. Add the coconut, salt and 8 fl oz (225ml) of water. Bring to a boil. (This much of the recipe may be made several hours ahead of time.) Add the mussels. Mix well and bring to a boil. Cover tightly. Lower heat slightly and let mussels steam for 6–10 minutes or until they open up. Serve immediately.

Prawns with courgettes

Jhinga aur ghia

We do not have courgettes in India but we do have a variety of similar squashes which are often cooked with prawns and other seafood. Here is one such combination. I prefer to use relatively small courgettes that weigh about $\frac{1}{4}$ lb (110g) each. If you can only get larger ones, just cut them appropriately so that each piece is just a little larger than a prawn.

I like to serve these prawns with 'Spiced basmati rice' (page 148) or 'Plain long grain rice' (page 146) and 'Red split lentils' (page 122).

Serves 4:

$\frac{3}{4}$ lb (350g) courgettes (see note above)

$1\frac{1}{4}$ teaspoons salt

$\frac{3}{4}$ lb (350g) peeled, good quality prawns, defrosted

5 tablespoons vegetable oil

6 cloves garlic, peeled and very finely chopped

3 oz (75g) finely chopped fresh coriander (weight without lower stems and roots)

1 fresh, hot green chilli, finely chopped

$\frac{1}{2}$ teaspoon ground turmeric

$1\frac{1}{2}$ teaspoons ground cumin seeds

$\frac{1}{4}$ teaspoon cayenne

3 small tinned tomatoes, finely chopped, plus 4 fl oz (125ml) of liquid in tin

1 teaspoon very finely grated fresh ginger

1 tablespoon lemon juice

Scrub the courgettes and trim them. Now cut them in 4 slices lengthwise. Cut each slice, lengthwise, into 4 long strips. Cut the strips into thirds, crosswise. Put the courgettes in a bowl. Sprinkle $\frac{1}{4}$ teaspoon salt over the pieces. Toss to mix and set aside for 30–40 minutes. Drain and pat dry.

Put the prawns on kitchen paper and dry them off as well.

Heat the oil in a wide pot or a frying pan over a medium-high flame. When hot, put in the chopped garlic. Stir and fry until the garlic pieces turn a medium brown colour. Put in the courgettes, coriander, green chilli, turmeric, cumin, cayenne, tomatoes and their liquid, ginger, lemon juice, and remaining 1 teaspoon salt. Stir to mix and bring to a simmer. Add the prawns and stir them in. Cover, turn heat to low and simmer for 3 minutes.

Uncover, turn the heat to medium and boil away from the liquid, if there is any, so that you are left with a thick sauce.

Prawns in a dark sauce

Rasedar jhinga

I like to serve these prawns with plain basmati rice, 'Cauliflower and potatoes' (page 109), and 'Tomato, onion, and green coriander relish' (page 172).

Serves 4:

3 oz (75g) onion, peeled and coarsely chopped

5 cloves garlic, peeled

A 1 inch (2.5cm) cube of fresh ginger, peeled and coarsely chopped

3 tablespoons plus $\frac{1}{2}$ pint (275ml) water

4 tablespoons vegetable oil

A 1 inch (2.5cm) stick of cinnamon

6 whole cardamom pods

2 bay leaves

2 teaspoons ground cumin seeds

1 teaspoon ground coriander seeds

6 oz (175g) tomatoes, peeled (see page 29) and very finely chopped

5 tablespoons plain yoghurt

$\frac{1}{2}$ teaspoon ground turmeric

$\frac{1}{4}$–$\frac{1}{2}$ teaspoon cayenne pepper

About $\frac{3}{4}$ teaspoon salt

$\frac{3}{4}$ lb (350g) peeled, good quality prawns, defrosted and patted dry

$\frac{1}{4}$ teaspoon garam masala (page 18)

2 tablespoons finely chopped fresh coriander

Put the onion, garlic, ginger, and 3 tablespoons water into the container of an electric blender and blend until you have a paste.

Heat the oil in an 8–9 inch (20–23cm) wide pot over a medium-high flame. When hot, put in the cinnamon, cardamom, and bay leaves. Stir for 3–4 seconds. Now put in the paste from the blender. Stir and fry for about 5 minutes or until the paste turns a light brown colour. Add the ground cumin and coriander. Stir and fry for 30 seconds. Put in the tomatoes. Stir and keep frying until the paste has a nice reddish-brown look to it. Now put in 1 tablespoon of the yoghurt. Stir and fry for 10–15 seconds or until the yoghurt is incorporated into the sauce. Add all the yoghurt this way, 1 tablespoon at a time. Put in the turmeric and cayenne and stir for a minute. Now put in $\frac{1}{2}$ pint (275ml) water, the salt, and the prawns. Stir to mix and bring to a boil over a medium-high flame. Stir and cook over this medium-high flame for about 5 minutes or until you have a good, thick sauce. Do not overcook the prawns. Sprinkle the *garam masala* over the top and mix. Serve garnished with fresh coriander.

N.B. The large whole spices are not meant to be eaten.

Halibut with cauliflower

Macchi aur phool gobi

All you need to serve with this dish is some rice and a relish.

Serves 4–6:

A 1 inch (2.5cm) thick halibut steak, weighing about 2 lb (900g) (2 smaller steaks of equal thickness will do)

$1\frac{1}{2}$ teaspoons ground cumin seeds

$1\frac{1}{2}$ teaspoons ground coriander seeds

$\frac{1}{2}$ teaspoon ground turmeric

About $\frac{1}{2}$ teaspoon cayenne pepper

$1\frac{1}{2}$ teaspoons salt

4 oz (110g) onion, peeled and coarsely chopped

Two 1 inch (2.5cm) cubes of fresh ginger, peeled and coarsely chopped

1–2 fresh hot green chillies, roughly cut into 3–4 pieces each

3 tablespoons plus $\frac{3}{4}$ pint (425ml) water

7 tablespoons vegetable oil

$\frac{3}{4}$ lb (350g) flowerets from a cauliflower head, each about 2 inches (5cm) in length and about 1 inch (2.5cm) across at the top

6 tablespoons plain yoghurt

Freshly ground black pepper

Have the fishmonger cut the halibut steak into pieces that are approximately 2 by $1\frac{1}{2}$ by 1 inches (5 by 4 by 2.5cm). Alternatively, you may do this yourself at home with a heavy cleaver that can hack through the bone. Leave the skin on.

Put the fish pieces in a bowl. Sprinkle $\frac{1}{2}$ teaspoon of the cumin, $\frac{1}{2}$ teaspoon of the coriander, $\frac{1}{4}$ teaspoon of the turmeric, $\frac{1}{4}$ teaspoon of the cayenne, and $\frac{1}{2}$ teaspoon of the salt over them. Toss to mix evenly. Set aside for $\frac{1}{2}$–1 hour.

Put the onion, ginger, green chillies, and 3 tablespoons water into the container of an electric blender. Blend until you have a paste.

Heat 6 tablespoons of the oil in a 12 inch (30cm), preferably non-stick, sauté pan or deep frying pan over a medium flame. When hot, put in the cauliflower flowerets. Stir and fry them until they are very lightly browned. Remove with a slotted spoon and set aside in a bowl. Sprinkle $\frac{1}{4}$ teaspoon salt and some black pepper over the cauliflower. Toss to mix.

Put the fish pieces into the same pan in a single layer and brown lightly on both sides. Do not let the fish cook through. Remove the fish pieces carefully and keep them in a plate.

Add another tablespoon of oil to the pan and heat on a medium-high flame. When hot, put in the paste from the blender. Stir and fry the paste until it turns a light brown colour. Now add the remaining 1 teaspoon cumin, 1 teaspoon coriander, $\frac{1}{8}$–$\frac{1}{4}$ teaspoon cayenne, and $\frac{3}{4}$ teaspoon salt. Stir and fry for a minute. Put in 1 tablespoon of the yoghurt. Stir and fry it for about 30 seconds or until it is incorporated into the paste. Add all the yoghurt this way, 1 tablespoon at a time. Now pour in $\frac{3}{4}$ pint (425ml) water, stir and bring to a simmer. Simmer on medium heat for 2 minutes. Gently put in the fish pieces and the cauliflower. Cover partially and cook on medium heat for about 5 minutes or until the fish is cooked through and the cauliflower is tender. Spoon the sauce over the fish and vegetables several times during this period.

Fried plaice fillets

Tali hui macchi

This is one of the simpler fish dishes served in many parts of India, with each area using its own local fish. The breading is, of course, a Western influence. Wedges of lemon or some tomato ketchup may be served on the side.

Serves 4:

1½ lb (700g) plaice fillets with dark skin removed

¾ teaspoon salt

Freshly ground black pepper

1½ teaspoons ground cumin seeds

½ teaspoon ground turmeric

½ teaspoon cayenne pepper

2 tablespoons very finely chopped fresh green coriander (use parsley as a substitute)

2 large eggs

6 oz (175g) fresh breadcrumbs

Vegetable oil for shallow frying (enough to have ½ inch (1cm) in frying pan)

Cut the fish fillet crosswise and at a slight diagonal, into ¾ inch (2cm) wide strips. Lay the strips on a plate and sprinkle them on both sides with the salt, pepper, cumin, turmeric, cayenne, and fresh coriander. Pat down the spices so they adhere to the fish. Set aside for 15 minutes.

Break the eggs into a deep plate. Add 4 teaspoons water and beat lightly. Spread the breadcrumbs out in a second plate. Dip the fish pieces first in the egg and then in the crumbs to coat evenly.

Put about ½ inch (1cm) of oil in a large frying pan and heat over a medium flame. When hot, put in as many pieces of fish as the pan will hold easily. Fry for 2–3 minutes on each side or until golden brown. Drain on kitchen paper. Fry all the fish strips this way and serve hot.

Haddock baked in a yoghurt sauce

Dahi wali macchi

This is one of my favourite fish dishes – and it is so easy to put together. All you have to do is combine the ingredients in a baking dish and bake for about 30 minutes. You do have to boil down the sauce later but that takes just an additional 5 minutes. I like to serve this dish with 'Mushroom pullao' (page 152) and 'Spinach with potatoes' (page 116).

If you cannot get haddock, use any other, thick-cut fish such as cod or halibut.

Serves 4–6:

6 oz (175g) onions, peeled

2 lb (1kg approx) 1 inch (2.5cm) thick fresh haddock fillets

15 fl oz (425ml) plain yoghurt

2 tablespoons lemon juice

1 teaspoon sugar

1½ teaspoons salt

¼ teaspoon coarsely ground black pepper

2 teaspoons ground cumin seeds

2 tablespoons ground coriander seeds

¼ teaspoon garam masala (page 18)

½–¾ teaspoon cayenne pepper

1 teaspoon peeled and finely grated fresh ginger

3 tablespoons vegetable oil

1½ oz (40g) unsalted cold butter, cut into pats

Preheat oven to gas mark 5, 375°F (190°C).

Cut the onions into ⅛ inch (3mm) thick slices and line a large baking dish with them. (The dish should be large enough to hold the fish in a single layer. It need not be more than 1½ inches (4cm) in depth.) Cut the fish fillets, crosswise, into 3 inch (7.5cm) long segments and lay them over the onions.

Put the yoghurt into a bowl. Beat it lightly. Add the lemon juice, sugar, salt, black pepper, cumin, coriander, *garam masala*, cayenne, and ginger. Mix well. Add the oil and mix again. Pour this sauce over the fish, making sure that some of it goes under the pieces as well. Cover (with aluminium foil, if necessary) and bake in the upper third of the oven for 30 minutes or until the fish is just done.

Carefully, pour out all the liquid from the baking dish into a small saucepan. (Keep the fish covered and in a warm place.) The sauce will look thin and 'separated'. Bring it to a boil. Boil rapidly until there are about 12 fl oz (350ml) of sauce left. Take the saucepan off the heat. Put in the pieces of butter and beat them in with a fork. As soon as the butter has melted, pour the sauce over the fish and serve.

(You may also serve the dish cold, after it has been refrigerated overnight. This is not very traditional but we love it that way, with a green salad on the side.)

Cod steaks in a spicy tomato sauce

Timatar wali macchi

I like to serve this with 'Rice with peas' (page 149) and 'Spinach cooked with onions' (page 115).

Serves 4:

4 cod steaks, weighing about 2 lb (1kg approx.)

$1\frac{1}{4}$ teaspoons salt

$\frac{1}{2}$ teaspoon cayenne pepper

$\frac{1}{4}$ teaspoon ground turmeric

9 tablespoons vegetable oil

1 teaspoon whole fennel seeds

1 teaspoon whole mustard seeds

6 oz (175g) onions, peeled and finely chopped

2 cloves garlic, peeled and finely chopped

2 teaspoons ground cumin seeds

14 oz (400g) tin of tomatoes, with the tomatoes chopped up

$\frac{1}{2}$ teaspoon ground, roasted cumin seeds (see page 17), optional

$\frac{1}{4}$ teaspoon garam masala (page 18)

Pat the fish steaks dry with kitchen paper. Rub them, on both sides, with $\frac{1}{4}$ teaspoon of the salt, $\frac{1}{4}$ teaspoon of the cayenne, and $\frac{1}{4}$ teaspoon turmeric. Set aside for 30 minutes.

Heat 4 tablespoons of the oil in a saucepan over medium heat. When hot, put in the fennel and mustard seeds. As soon as the mustard seeds begin to pop (this just takes a few seconds), put in the onions and garlic. Stir and fry until the onions turn slightly brown. Now put in the cumin, 1 teaspoon salt and $\frac{1}{4}$ teaspoon cayenne. Stir once and put in the tomatoes and their liquid, the roasted cumin, and *garam masala*. Bring to a boil. Cover, turn heat to low, and simmer gently for 15 minutes.

Meanwhile, preheat the oven to gas mark 4, 350°F (180°C).

Put the remaining 5 tablespoons of oil in a large, preferably non-stick frying pan and heat over a medium-high flame. When hot, put in the fish steaks and brown on both sides. Do not cook the fish through. Put the steaks in a baking dish. Pour the cooked tomato sauce over the fish and bake, uncovered, for 15 minutes or until the fish is done.

Grilled mackerel with lemon and fresh coriander

Hare masale wali macchi

Indian mackerel seem to me to be much plumper than their English counterparts. Perhaps the warmer waters make them lazier. Goan fishermen on India's west coast roast them right on the beach over smouldering rice straws. The blackened skin is then peeled away and the now pristine, skinless fish served with a simple vinegar dressing. A good fresh mackerel needs nothing more.

Further up the same coast, in large cities like Bombay, the fish is marinaded first in a dressing of lemon juice and fresh green coriander and then fried or grilled. Here is the Bombay recipe. I often serve it with 'Mushroom pullao' (page 152) and 'Cabbage with peas' (page 105).

Serves 2:

- 2 medium-sized, whole mackerel, about 1½ lb (700g) in all, cleaned
- 3 tablespoons very finely chopped fresh green coriander
- ½–1 fresh, hot green chilli, finely chopped
- 1 tablespoon lemon juice
- ½ teaspoon salt
- Freshly ground black pepper
- 2 oz (50g) unsalted butter, cut into pats

Cut the heads off the mackerel. Split them all the way down the stomach and then lay them out flat, skin side up, on a firm surface.

Now bone the fish this way: Press down firmly with the heel of your hand all along the backbone. This should loosen the bone from the flesh somewhat. Now turn the fish over so the skin side is down. Work your fingers (or else use a knife) under the bones to prise them away from the fish. Cut two to three shallow diagonal slashes on the skin side of each fish.

Combine the fresh coriander, chilli, lemon juice, salt and black pepper, in a bowl. Mix well. Rub this mixture all over the fish. Set aside for 45 minutes.

Heat the grill. Put the fish in the grill pan, with the rack removed, skin side up, and dot with half the butter. Grill, 4 inches (10cm) away from the flame, for about 5 minutes. Turn the fish over, dot with the remaining butter and grill for 4 minutes or until golden brown.

VEGETABLES

I love all vegetables – from shiny purple aubergines that can be fried very simply with a light dusting of turmeric and cayenne to the humble potato which, in India, is cooked in at least a thousand different ways including one in which black pepper is the main seasoning.

As many Indians are vegetarians, we have, over the years, worked out a great variety of ways to cook our everyday vegetables such as cabbages, green beans, beetroots and carrots. Sometimes the vegetables are cut into shreds or slices and quickly stir-fried with whole spices such as cumin and mustard seeds. These are referred to as 'dry' vegetables and rarely have even the glimmer of a sauce. At other times we may cook root vegetables in a thick ginger-garlic sauce or with tomatoes. Such dishes are referred to as 'wet' dishes because of the sauce. They are generally served in small, individual bowls. Both 'dry' and 'wet' dishes may be served with rice or Indian breads.

For those of you who are vegetarians – or want to cut down on your meat intake – you can make perfectly balanced meals by picking two or three vegetables from this chapter and then adding a pulse dish, a rice or bread and a yoghurt relish.

Fried aubergine slices

Tala hua baigan

This is one of the simplest ways of cooking aubergines in India. Ideally, the frying should be done at the very last minute and the melt-in-the-mouth slices served as soon as they come out of the hot oil. Sometimes I arrange these slices, like petals, around a roast leg of lamb. They can, of course, be served with any Indian meal.

Left over aubergine slices, if there are any, may be heated together with any leftover, Indian-style meat the following day. The combination makes for a new dish and is very good.

Serves 4–6:

$1\frac{1}{4}$ lb (560g) aubergine

About 1 teaspoon salt

$\frac{1}{2}$ teaspoon ground turmeric

$\frac{1}{8}$–$\frac{1}{2}$ teaspoon ground cayenne pepper

Some freshly ground black pepper

Vegetable oil for shallow frying

6–8 lemon wedges

Cut the aubergine into quarters, lengthwise, and then cut, crosswise, into $\frac{1}{2}$ inch (1cm) thick wedges.

Mix the salt, turmeric, cayenne, and black pepper in a small bowl. Sprinkle this combination over the aubergines and mix well.

Heat about $\frac{1}{3}$ inch (1cm) of oil in a 8–9 inch (20–23cm) frying pan over a medium flame. When hot, put in as many aubergine slices as the pan will hold in a single layer. Fry until reddish-gold on one side. Turn the slices and fry them on their second side. Remove with a slotted spoon and spread out on a plate lined with kitchen paper. Do a second batch, adding more oil, if you need to.

Serve with lemon wedges.

The Lake Palace Hotel's
Aubergine cooked in the pickling style

Baigan achari

Right in the centre of a lake in the formerly royal city of Udaipur is a summer palace, now converted, as most Indian palaces seem fated to be, into a spectacular hotel. This recipe comes from its master chef, Shankerlal, and in its finished effect is not unlike a spicy ratatouille. It is an exquisite dish. While *Kalonji* – black onion seeds – do give this dish its special 'pickled' taste, you may use whole cumin seeds instead.

I love to eat this dish with a hearty lamb stew, such as *Rogan josh* ('Red lamb stew', page 51) and a bread (such as *parathas*). If you do not feel like an all-Indian meal, you could serve it with a leg of roast lamb and plain rice. I think it also tastes excellent cold. I often dole out individual portions on lettuce leaves and serve them as a first course. Sometimes I serve this dish for lunch with cold chicken, cold lamb, or sliced ham.

Serves 6:

A 1 inch (2.5cm) cube of fresh ginger, peeled and coarsely chopped

6 large cloves of garlic, peeled

2 fl oz (55ml) water

$1\frac{3}{4}$ lb (800g) aubergines (large or small variety)

2 fl oz (55ml) water

About 12 fl oz (350ml) vegetable oil

1 teaspoon whole fennel seeds

$\frac{1}{2}$ teaspoon kalonji or whole cumin seeds

$\frac{3}{4}$ lb (350g) tomatoes, peeled (see page 29) and finely chopped

1 tablespoon ground coriander seeds

$\frac{1}{4}$ teaspoon ground turmeric

$\frac{1}{3}$ teaspoon cayenne pepper (more, if you like)

About $1\frac{1}{4}$ teaspoon salt

Put the ginger and garlic into the container of an electric blender or food processor. Add 2 fl oz (55ml) of water and blend until fairly smooth.

Cut the aubergine into slices or wedges that are $\frac{3}{4}$ inch (2cm) thick and about $1\frac{1}{2}$–2 inches (4–5cm) long.

Set a sieve over a bowl.

Heat 4 fl oz (125ml) of oil in a deep, 10–12 inch (25–30cm) frying pan or saucepan over a medium-high flame. When hot, put in as many aubergine slices as the pan will hold in a single layer. Let them turn a reddish-brown colour. Turn them over and brown the opposite sides. Remove the slices and put them in the sieve. Add another 4 fl oz (125ml) of oil to the frying pan and heat it. Brown a second batch of aubergine slices, just as you did the first. You will probably need to do three batches, adding fresh oil to the frying pan each time.

(You may now turn off the heat under the frying pan and let the aubergine drain for about an hour or you may proceed immediately with the next step. The idea is to get rid of some of the oil that aubergines absorb so easily. You will achieve this end either way, though I do think it helps slightly to get rid of the oil at the earlier stage.)

Put 3 tablespoons of oil in the frying pan and heat it over a medium flame. When hot, put in the fennel seeds and kalonji, or whole cumin. As soon as the fennel seeds turn a few shades darker (this takes just a few seconds), put in the chopped tomato, the ginger-garlic mixture, coriander, turmeric, cayenne and salt. Stir and cook for 5–6 minutes, breaking the tomato pieces with the back of a slotted spoon. Turn the heat up slightly and continue to stir and cook until the spice mixture gets thick and pastelike.

Now put in the fried aubergine slices and mix gently. Cook on medium low heat for about 5 minutes, stirring very gently as you do so. Cover the pan, turn heat to very low and cook another 5–10 minutes if you think it is necessary.

Oil will have collected at the bottom of the frying pan. Use a slotted spoon to lift the aubergine out of this oil when you serve.

You could also serve this dish cold, almost as if it were a salad. In that case, store it with all its oil in the refrigerator. Take it out of the oil only when you serve.

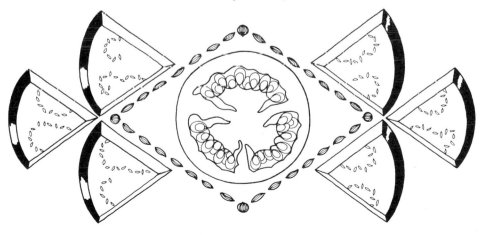

Gujerati-style green beans

Gujerati sem

Here is a very simple, yet delicious way to cook green beans. This dish goes well both with Indian meals and with grilled and roasted meats (I like it with sausages). Gujeratis often cook green vegetables with a little baking soda in order to preserve their bright colour. I am told that this kills the vitamins. So I blanch the beans and rinse them out quickly under cold running water instead. This works equally well. I generally do the blanching and rinsing quite a bit ahead of time and do the final cooking just before we sit down to eat.

If you do not want the beans to be hot, either do without the red chilli or else discard all its seeds and use just the skin for flavour.

Serves 4:

1 lb (450g) fresh green French beans

4 tablespoons vegetable oil

1 tablespoon whole black mustard seeds

4 cloves garlic, peeled and very finely chopped

½–1 hot, dried red chilli, coarsely crushed in a mortar

1 teaspoon salt

½ teaspoon sugar

Freshly ground black pepper

Trim the beans and cut them into 1 inch (2.5cm) lengths. Blanch the beans by dropping them into a pot of boiling water and boiling rapidly for 3–4 minutes or until they are just tender. Drain immediately in a colander and rinse under cold, running water. Set aside.

Heat the oil in a large frying pan over a medium flame. When hot, put in the mustard seeds. As soon as the mustard seeds begin to pop, put in the garlic. Stir the garlic pieces around until they turn light brown. Put in the crushed red chilli and stir for a few seconds. Put in the green beans, salt, and sugar. Stir to mix. Turn the heat to medium-low. Stir and cook the beans for 7–8 minutes or until they have absorbed the flavour of the spices. Add the black pepper, mix, and serve.

Spicy green beans

Masaledar sem

These green beans may, of course, be served with an Indian dinner. But they could perk up a simple meal of roast chicken, pork chops or meat loaf as well. They are tart and hot and would complement the plainest of everyday foods with their zesty blend of flavours. Another good thing about them – they may be made ahead of time and reheated.

Serves 6:

$1\frac{1}{2}$ lb (700g) fresh green French beans

A piece of fresh ginger, about $1\frac{1}{2}$ inches (4cm) long and 1 inch (2.5cm) thick, peeled and coarsely chopped

10 cloves of garlic, peeled

12 fl oz (350ml) water

5 tablespoons vegetable oil

2 teaspoons whole cumin seeds

1 whole, dried hot red chilli, lightly crushed in a mortar

2 teaspoons ground coriander seeds

$\frac{1}{2}$ lb (225g) tomatoes, peeled (see page 29 and finely chopped

About $1\frac{1}{4}$ teaspoons salt

3 tablespoons lemon juice – or to taste

1 teaspoon ground, roasted cumin seeds (see page 17)

Freshly ground black pepper

Trim the green beans and cut them, crosswise, at $\frac{1}{4}$ inch (5mm) intervals. Put the ginger and garlic into the container of an electric blender or food processor. Add 4 fl oz (125ml) of the measured water and blend until fairly smooth.

Heat the oil in a wide, heavy saucepan over a medium flame. When hot, put in the cumin seeds. Five seconds later, put in the crushed chilli. As soon as it darkens, pour in the ginger-garlic paste. Stir and cook for about a minute. Put in the coriander. Stir a few times. Now put in the chopped tomatoes. Stir and cook for about 2 minutes, mashing up the tomato pieces with the back of a slotted spoon as you do so. Put in the beans, salt, and the remaining water. Bring to simmer. Cover, turn heat to low and cook for about 8–10 minutes or until the beans are tender. Remove the cover. Add the lemon juice, roasted cumin, and a generous amount of freshly ground pepper. Turn heat up and boil away all of the liquid, stirring the beans gently as you do so.

Beetroot with onions

Shorvedar chukander

I love beetroot, in almost any form. Even people who do not have a weakness for this particular root vegetable, manage to succumb to the charms of this recipe. It is a kind of stew, thickened by the onions floating around in it and somewhat tart in flavour because of the tomatoes it contains. As there is a fair amount of sauce, I frequently serve it with 'Beef baked with yoghurt and black pepper' (page 50), a somewhat dry dish, and with 'Tomato, cucumber and green coriander relish' (page 172). *Chapatis* are the ideal bread to serve with this meal, though plain rice would also taste good.

Serves 3–4:

¾ lb (350g) raw beetroot (weight without stems and leaves)

4 tablespoons vegetable oil

1 teaspoon whole cumin seeds

1 clove garlic, peeled and very finely chopped

4 oz (110g) onion, peeled and coarsely chopped

1 teaspoon plain flour

⅛–½ teaspoon cayenne pepper

½ lb (225g) tomatoes, peeled (see page 29) and very finely chopped

1 teaspoon salt

½ pint (275ml) water

Peel the beetroot and cut them into wedges. A medium-sized beetroot, about 2 inches (5cm) in length, should, for example, be cut into 6 wedges.

Heat the oil in a medium-sized pot over a medium flame. When hot, put in the cumin seeds. Let them sizzle for 5 seconds. Put in the garlic. Stir and fry until the garlic pieces turn golden. Put in the onion. Stir and fry for 2 minutes. Put in the flour and cayenne. Stir and fry for a minute. Now put in the beetroot, the tomatoes, salt, and ½ pint (275ml) water. Bring to a simmer. Cover, turn heat to low and simmer 30 minutes or until beetroot are tender. Remove lid, turn up heat to medium, and cook uncovered for about 7 minutes or until the sauce has thickened slightly.

This dish may be made ahead of time and reheated.

Cabbage with peas

Bund gobi aur matar

Here is a simple cabbage dish that you could serve just as easily with grilled pork chops as with an Indian meal.

Serves 4:

1–1¼ lb (500g approx) green English cabbage

5 oz (150g) frozen peas

5 tablespoons vegetable oil

2 teaspoons whole cumin seeds

2 bay leaves

¼ teaspoon ground turmeric

¼ teaspoon cayenne pepper

1 fresh hot green chilli, very finely chopped

¾ teaspoon salt

¾ teaspoon sugar

¼ teaspoon garam masala (see page 18)

Core the cabbage and cut it into very fine, long shreds. Put the peas in a strainer and hold them under warm, running water until they separate.

Heat the oil in a wide pot over a medium-high flame. When hot, put in the cumin seeds and bay leaves. As soon as the bay leaves begin to take on colour – this just takes a few seconds – put in the cabbage and peas and stir them about for 30 seconds. Add the turmeric and cayenne. Stir to mix. Cover, turn heat to low and cook for 5 minutes or until vegetables are just tender. Add the green chilli, salt and sugar. Stir to mix. Cover and cook on low heat another 2–3 minutes. Remove cover and sprinkle in the *garam masala*. Stir gently and mix.

Remove bay leaves before serving.

Gujerati-style cabbage with carrots

Sambhara

This is the kind of everyday vegetable dish that is served in many homes in the state of Gujerat. It cooks quickly and may be served as well with pork chops as with an Indian meal.

Serves 4–6:

¾ lb (350g) green English cabbage
¾ lb (350g) carrots
½–1 fresh, hot green chilli
4 tablespoons vegetable oil
A pinch of ground asafetida (optional)
1 tablespoon whole black mustard seeds
1 whole, hot dried red chilli
About 1¼ teaspoons salt
½ teaspoon sugar
4 heaped tablespoons chopped fresh green coriander
1 tablespoon lemon juice

Core the cabbage and cut it into fine, long shreds. Peel the carrots and grate them coarsely. Cut the green chilli into thin, long strips.

Heat the oil in a wide, casserole-type pot over a medium-high flame. When hot, put in the asafetida. A second later, put in the mustard seeds. As soon as the mustard seeds begin to pop (this takes just a few seconds), put in the dried red chilli. Stir once. The chilli should turn dark red in seconds. Now put in the cabbage, carrots and green chilli. Turn the heat down to medium and stir the vegetables around for half a minute. Add the salt, sugar and green coriander. Stir and cook for another 5 minutes or until vegetables are just done and retain some of their crispness. Add the lemon juice. Stir to mix.

(Remove the whole red chilli before serving to those unfamiliar with Indian foods.)

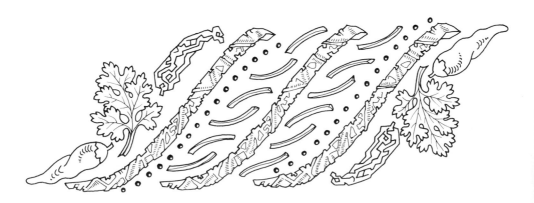

Carrots, peas, and potatoes, flavoured with cumin

Gajar, matar, aur gobi ki bhaji

Here is a simple, quick-cooking dish. Ideally, it should be made in an Indian *karhai* but if you do not have one, a large frying pan or sauté pan will do. The vegetables are cooked in a Bengali style but could easily accompany a roast chicken or grilled sausages.

Serves 6:

6 oz (175g) carrots

6 oz (175g) potatoes that have been boiled, drained and cooled

6 oz (175g) onions

1 spring onion

3 tablespoons mustard oil (another vegetable oil may be substituted)

1½ teaspoons whole cumin seeds

2 whole, dried hot red chillies

6 oz (175g) shelled peas

About 1 teaspoon salt

¼ teaspoon sugar

Peel the carrot and cut it first into ½ inch (1cm) thick diagonal slices and then into ½ inch (1cm) dice.

Peel the potato and cut it into ½ inch (1cm) dice. Peel the onion and chop it coarsely. Cut the spring onion into very, very thin slices, all the way to the end of its green section.

Heat the oil in a large frying pan over a medium flame. When hot, put in the cumin seeds. Let them sizzle for 3–4 seconds. Now put in the whole chillies and stir them about for 3–4 seconds. Put in the chopped onion. Stir and cook for 5 minutes or until onion pieces turn translucent. Put in the carrots and peas. Stir them about for a minute. Cover, turn heat to low, and cook for about 5 minutes or until vegetables are tender. Uncover and turn heat up slightly. Add the potatoes, salt, and sugar. Stir and cook another 2–3 minutes. Add the spring onion. Stir and cook for 30 seconds.

N.B. Remove the whole chillies before serving.

Cauliflower with onion and tomato
Phool gobi ki bhaji

A good all-round vegetable dish that goes well with most Indian meat dishes.

Serves 6:

Two medium-sized cauliflowers, about 2¼ lb (1kg) (you need about 1 lb 10 oz (725g) of flowerets)

3 oz (75g) onion, peeled and coarsely chopped

Two 1 inch (2.5cm) cubes of fresh ginger, peeled and coarsely chopped

7 tablespoons water

5 tablespoons vegetable oil

6 cloves garlic, peeled and very finely chopped

1 teaspoon ground cumin seeds

1 teaspoon ground coriander seeds

5–6 oz (150–175g) tomatoes, peeled (see page 29) and finely chopped

½ teaspoon ground turmeric

⅛–½ teaspoon cayenne pepper

½–1 fresh hot green chilli, finely chopped

1 tablespoon lemon juice

1¾ teaspoons salt

¼ teaspoon garam masala

Break up the cauliflower into flowerets that are about 1½ inches (4cm) across at the head and 1½–2 inches (4–5cm) in length. Let them soak in a bowl of water for 30 minutes. Drain.

Put the onion and ginger into the container of an electric blender along with 4 tablespoons of the water. Blend until you have a paste.

Heat the oil in a 9–10 inch (23–25cm) wide pot or deep frying pan over a medium-high flame. When hot, put in the garlic. Stir and fry until the pieces turn a medium-brown colour. Put in the cauliflower. Stir and fry for about 2 minutes or until the cauliflower pieces pick up a few brown spots. Remove the cauliflower with a slotted spoon and put it in a bowl. Put the onion–ginger mixture into the same pot. Stir and fry it for a minute. Now put in the cumin, coriander, and tomato. Stir and fry this mixture until it turns a medium brown colour. If it starts to catch, turn the heat down slightly and sprinkle in a tablespoon of water. Then keep frying until you have the right colour. Add the turmeric, cayenne, green chilli, lemon juice, and salt. Give a few good stirs and turn heat to low. Now put in the cauliflower and any possible liquid in the cauliflower bowl. Stir gently to mix. Add 3 tablespoons water, stir again and bring to a simmer. Cover and cook on gentle heat, stirring now and then, for 5–10 minutes or until cauliflower is just done. Remove lid and sprinkle *garam masala* over the top. Stir to mix.

Cauliflower with potatoes
Phool gobi aur aloo ki bhaji

This is the kind of comforting 'homey' dish that most North Indians enjoy. It has no sauce and is generally eaten with a bread. I like to serve *Shahi korma* (page 56) or Tandoori chicken (page 66) with it.

Serves 4–6:
½ lb (225g) potatoes
1 medium-sized cauliflower (you need 1 lb (450g) of flowerets)
5 tablespoons vegetable oil
1 teaspoon whole cumin seeds
1 teaspoon ground cumin seeds
½ teaspoon ground coriander seeds
¼ teaspoon ground turmeric
¼ teaspoon cayenne pepper
½–1 fresh, hot green chilli, very finely chopped
½ teaspoon ground roasted cumin seeds (see page 17)
1 teaspoon salt
Freshly ground black pepper

Boil the potatoes in their jackets and allow them to cool completely. (Day-old cooked potatoes that have been refrigerated work very well for this dish.) Peel the potatoes and cut them into ¾ inch (2cm) dice.

Break up the cauliflower into chunky flowerets, about 1½ inches (4cm) across at the head and about 1½ inches (4cm) long. Soak the flowerets in a bowl of water for 30 minutes. Drain.

Heat the oil in a large, preferably non-stick frying pan over a medium flame. When hot, put in the whole cumin seeds. Let the seeds sizzle for 3–4 seconds. Now put in the cauliflower and stir it about for 2 minutes. Let the cauliflower brown in spots. Cover, turn heat to low and simmer for about 4–6 minutes or until cauliflower is almost done but still has a hint of crispness left. Put in the diced potatoes, ground cumin, coriander, turmeric, cayenne, green chilli, ground roasted cumin, salt, and some black pepper. Stir gently to mix. Continue to cook uncovered on low heat for another 3 minutes or until potatoes are heated through. Stir gently as you do so.

Cauliflower with fennel and mustard seeds
Baghari phool gobi

You need about 2 medium-sized cauliflowers for this dish or one large one. When the flowerets have all been cut, you should end up with about 2 lb of the vegetable.

You could serve this dish with 'Chicken in a red pepper sauce' (page 79) and rice.

Serves 6:

1 large or 2 medium-sized cauliflowers (see note above)
7 tablespoons vegetable oil
2 teaspoons whole fennel seeds
1 tablespoon whole black mustard seeds
1 tablespoon very finely chopped garlic
$\frac{1}{4}$ teaspoon ground turmeric
$\frac{1}{4}-\frac{1}{3}$ teaspoon cayenne pepper
About $1\frac{1}{2}$ teaspoons salt
4 tablespoons water

Cut the cauliflower into delicate flowerets that are no longer than 2 inches (5cm), no wider at the head than an inch and about $\frac{1}{3}$ inch (1cm approx) thick. Put them into a bowl of water for at least half an hour. Drain them just before you get ready to cook.

Heat the oil in a large, 10–12 inch (25–30cm) frying pan over a medium flame. When hot, put in the fennel and mustard seeds. As soon as the mustard seeds begin to pop, put in the finely chopped garlic. Stir and fry until the garlic pieces are lightly browned. Add the turmeric and cayenne. Stir once and quickly put in the cauliflower, salt, and about 4 tablespoons of water. Stir and cook on medium heat for 6–7 minutes or until cauliflower is just done. It should retain its crispness and there should be no liquid left. If the water evaporates before the cauliflower is done, add a little more.

(If your frying pan is smaller than the suggested size, the cauliflower will take longer to cook. In that case, it might be a good idea to cover it for 5 minutes.)

Mushrooms and potatoes, cooked with garlic and ginger

Rasedar khumbi aloo

This is one of those 'home-style' dishes that you rarely find in Indian restaurants. It is a thick, earthy stew that used to be made only when slim, monsoon mushrooms made a brief, seasonal appearance. Now, even in Indian cities you can buy cultivated white mushrooms all year round. Since these mushrooms come in a variety of sizes, you will have to use your own judgement about whether you should halve them, quarter them, or leave them whole. They should end up being about the same size as the diced potatoes.

You could serve this with 'Beef baked with yoghurt and black pepper' (page 50) and 'Gujerati carrot salad' (page 170).

Serves 4–6

9–10 oz (250–275g) potatoes

12 oz (350g) mushrooms

A 1 inch (2.5cm) piece of fresh ginger, peeled

6 large cloves garlic, peeled

3 tablespoons plus 8 fl oz (225ml) water

4 tablespoons vegetable oil

About 1 teaspoon salt

About $\frac{1}{3}$ teaspoon ground turmeric

1 teaspoon whole cumin seeds

3 whole cardamom pods

10 oz (275g) tomatoes, peeled (see page 29) and finely chopped

1 teaspoon ground cumin seeds

$\frac{1}{2}$ teaspoon ground coriander seeds

About $\frac{1}{4}$ teaspoon cayenne pepper

$\frac{1}{4}$ teaspoon garam masala (see page 18)

Optional garnish: 1 tablespoon finely chopped fresh coriander

Boil the potatoes in their jackets. Drain and peel them. Cut them into 1 inch (2.5cm) cubes.

Wipe the mushrooms with a damp cloth. Cut off the lower, woody part of the stems. Now, depending upon their size, halve or quarter the mushrooms, or, if they are small, leave them whole. They should be about the size of the diced potatoes.

Put the ginger and garlic into the container of a food processor or electric blender along with 3 tablespoons of water. Blend until you have a fine purée.

Put the diced potatoes in a bowl. Sprinkle about $\frac{1}{4}$ teaspoon salt and about $\frac{1}{8}$ teaspoon turmeric over them. Toss to mix and set aside.

Heat the oil in a heavy, wide, preferably non-stick pan over a medium flame. When hot, put in the potatoes. Stir and fry them until they are lightly browned on all sides. Remove potato pieces with a slotted spoon and set aside in a plate. Put whole cumin seeds and cardamom pods into the same pot. Stir them about for 3–4 seconds. Now put in the tomatoes, the ginger-garlic paste, the ground cumin and the ground coriander. Stir and fry until the paste becomes thick and the oil separates from it. Add $\frac{1}{4}$ teaspoon turmeric and the cayenne. Stir once or twice. Put in 8 fl oz water, the potatoes, mushrooms, and $\frac{3}{4}$ teaspoon salt. Stir to mix and bring to a simmer. Cover, turn heat to low and simmer for 5 minutes. Remove the cover and turn heat up slightly. Cook, stirring gently, until you have a thick sauce. Sprinkle in the *garam masala* and stir to mix. Taste for salt.

Serve garnished with fresh coriander.

N.B. The whole cardamom pods are not meant to be eaten.

Sweet and sour okra

Kutchhi bhindi

Here is an absolutely wonderful way to cook okra. It tastes best when made with young, tender pods.

It may be served with 'Lamb with onions' (page 46) and 'Mushroom pullao' (page 152).

Serves 4–6:

14 oz (400g) fresh, tender okra (bhindi)
7 medium-sized cloves of garlic, peeled
1 whole, dried hot red chilli (use half if you want it very mild)
7 tablespoons water
2 teaspoons ground cumin seeds
1 teaspoon ground coriander seeds
½ teaspoon ground turmeric
4 tablespoons vegetable oil
1 teaspoon whole cumin seeds
About 1 teaspoon salt
1 teaspoon sugar
About 4 teaspoons lemon juice

Rinse off the fresh okra and pat it dry. Trim the pods by cutting off the two ends. The top end is usually trimmed with a paring knife to leave a cone-shaped head. A tiny piece of the bottom is just snipped off. Cut the okra into ¾ inch (2cm) lengths.

Put the garlic and chilli into the container of an electric blender with 3 tablespoons of the water. Blend until you have a smooth paste.

Empty the paste into a small bowl. Add the ground cumin, coriander and turmeric. Mix.

Heat the oil in a 9 inch (23cm) frying pan or sauté pan over a medium flame. When hot, put in the whole cumin seeds. As soon as the cumin seeds begin to sizzle (this happens within a few seconds), turn the heat down a bit and pour in the spice mixture sitting in the small bowl. Stir and fry for about a minute. Now put in the okra, salt, sugar, lemon juice, and 4 tablespoons of water. Stir to mix and bring to a gentle simmer. Cover tightly and cook on low heat for about 10 minutes or until okra is tender. If your okra takes longer to cook, you might need to add just a little more water.

Potatoes with black pepper

Bengali aloo

We take black pepper so much for granted, sprinkling tiny amounts on most foods without much thought. Apart from its taste, black pepper has a very enticing perfume and a delicate tartness as well. These properties are drawn out when the spice is used in generous quantities – as in the French *steak au poivre* or in these very Bengali potatoes. The dish is simplicity itself to make and may be eaten just as easily with European foods as with Indian. You could also stick toothpicks into the potato pieces and serve them with drinks.

Serves 4:

1 lb 5 oz (600g) potatoes
4 tablespoons vegetable oil
About $\frac{3}{4}$ teaspoon salt
1–1$\frac{1}{2}$ teaspoons freshly ground black pepper (a slightly coarse grind is best)
2 tablespoons very finely chopped fresh coriander or parsley, optional

Boil the potatoes in their jackets and allow them to cool completely. (Day-old boiled potatoes that have been refrigerated work very well for this dish.) Peel the potatoes and cut them into $\frac{3}{4}$ inch (2cm) dice.

Heat the oil in a non-stick or very well seasoned frying pan over a medium flame. When hot, put in the potatoes and stir them around for a minute. Sprinkle in the salt and mix gently. Cover the potatoes and let them heat through on a medium-low flame for about 5 minutes. Stir them a few times during this period. Now add the black pepper and mix gently. Cook, uncovered, for another few minutes on a medium flame, stirring the potatoes every now and then and allowing them to brown slightly. Sprinkle in the fresh coriander, if you are using it. Mix and serve hot.

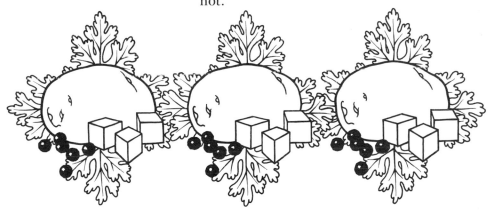

Potatoes with sesame seeds

Til ke aloo

Here is another of those easy, delicious dishes that you might enjoy both with Indian meals and with simple dinners of roasted and grilled meats.

Serves 6:

2 lb (1kg) potatoes

6 tablespoons vegetable oil

2 teaspoons whole cumin seeds

2 teaspoons whole black mustard seeds

2 tablespoons whole sesame seeds

About 2 teaspoons salt

$\frac{1}{8}$–$\frac{1}{2}$ teaspoon cayenne pepper

1 tablespoon lemon juice

Boil the potatoes in their jackets. Drain and cool them for 3–4 hours. Peel the potatoes and dice them into $\frac{3}{4}$ inch (2cm) cubes.

Heat the oil in a large, 10–12 inch (25–30cm) frying pan over a medium flame. (A non-stick or well-seasoned cast-iron frying pan would be ideal.) When the oil is very hot, put in the cumin seeds, mustard seeds and sesame seeds. As soon as the seeds begin to pop (this just takes a few seconds), put in the diced potatoes. Stir and fry the potatoes for about 5 minutes. Add the salt, cayenne and lemon juice. Stir and fry for another 3–4 minutes. I like the potatoes to have a few brown spots on them.

'Dry' potatoes with ginger and garlic

Sookhe aloo

Can you imagine cubes of potato encrusted with a spicy, crisply browned, ginger-garlic paste? Add to that a hint of fennel, if you want it. That is what these potatoes taste like. You could serve them with an Indian meal of *Kheema matar* ('Minced meat with peas', page 44), an Indian bread and a yoghurt relish, or you could serve them with grilled or roasted meats.

It is best to make this dish in a large, non-stick frying pan or a well-used cast-iron one.

Serves 4–5:
1 lb 6 oz (625g) potatoes
A piece of fresh ginger, about 2 by 1 by 1 inches (5 by 2.5 by 2.5cm), peeled and coarsely chopped
3 cloves garlic, peeled
3 tablespoons water
½ teaspoon ground turmeric
1 teaspoon salt
½ teaspoon cayenne pepper
5 tablespoons vegetable oil
1 teaspoon whole fennel seeds (optional)

Boil the potatoes in their jackets. Drain them and let them cool completely. Peel the potatoes and cut them into ¾–1 inch (2–2.5cm) dice.

Put the ginger, garlic, 3 tablespoons water, turmeric, salt, and cayenne into the container of a good processor or blender. Blend until you have a paste.

Heat the oil in a large, preferably non-stick frying pan over a medium flame. When hot, put in the fennel seeds. Let them sizzle for a few seconds. Now put in the ginger-garlic paste. Stir and fry for 2 minutes. Put in the potatoes. Stir and fry for 5–7 minutes over a medium-high flame or until the potatoes have a nice, golden-brown crust on them.

Spinach cooked with onions

Mughlai saag

I frequently serve this spinach with 'Chicken with cream' (page 74) and spiced basmati rice.

Serves 4:
2 lb (1kg) spinach, washed and trimmed
4 oz (110g) onions, peeled
4 tablespoons ghee or vegetable oil
½–1 fresh, hot green chilli, finely chopped
1 teaspoon very finely grated, peeled fresh ginger
About 1 teaspoon salt
½ teaspoon sugar
4 fl oz (125ml) water
¼ teaspoon garam masala (see page 18)

Cut the spinach, crosswise, into ½ inch (1cm) wide strips. Chop the onion finely.

Heat the *ghee* in a fairly large pot over a medium-high flame. When hot, put in the onions. Stir and fry for 3 minutes. Now put in the chopped spinach, green chilli, ginger, salt, and sugar. Stir and cook the spinach for 5 minutes. Add 4 fl oz (125ml) water and bring to a simmer. Cover tightly, turn heat to low, and cook for about 10 minutes. Uncover and boil away some of the extra liquid. Sprinkle *garam masala* over the top and mix.

Frozen spinach with potatoes

Saag aloo

In India, we combine potatoes with almost every grain, meat, and vegetable. Here is one of my favourite recipes. It may be served with *Rogan josh* ('Red lamb or beef stew', page 51) and an Indian bread or rice.

Serves 4–6:

20 oz (550g) (2 packets) frozen leaf spinach

½ pint (275ml) plus 2 tablespoons water

4 oz (110g) onions, peeled

5 tablespoons vegetable oil

A pinch of ground asafetida (optional)

2 teaspoons whole black mustard seeds

2 cloves garlic, peeled and finely chopped

18 oz (500g) potatoes, peeled and cut roughly into ¾–1 inch (2–2.5cm) cubes

¼ teaspoon cayenne pepper

1 teaspoon salt

Bring ½ pint (275ml) water to a boil in a saucepan. Put in the frozen spinach, cover, and cook the spinach until it is just done. Drain in a colander and rinse under cold water. Press out most of the liquid in the leaves (you do not have to be too thorough) and then chop them coarsely.

Cut the onions into half, lengthwise, and then crosswise into very thin slices.

Heat the oil in a heavy saucepan over a medium flame. When hot, put in the asafetida and then, a second later, the mustard seeds. As soon as the mustard seeds begin to pop (this just takes a few seconds), put in the onions and garlic. Stir and fry for 2 minutes. Put in the potatoes and cayenne. Stir and fry for a minutes. Now put in the spinach, salt, and 2 tablespoons water. Bring to a boil. Cover tightly, turn heat to very low and cook gently for 40 minutes or until the potatoes are tender. Stir a few times during the cooking period and make sure that there is always a little liquid in the pot.

Stewed tomatoes

Shorvedar timatar

It is best to make this dish in the summer, when tomatoes are plentiful. This is a 'wet' dish – it has a thinnish sauce – and should be served in individual bowls. You could eat it with 'Beef baked with yoghurt and black pepper' (page 50), 'Spicy baked chicken' (page 71) or 'Grilled mackerel with lemon and coriander' (page 96). Rice should be served on the side.

Serves 4:

1½ lb (700g) tomatoes

3 tablespoons vegetable oil

½ teaspoon whole cumin seeds

3 cloves garlic, peeled and very finely chopped

4 oz (110g) onion, peeled and chopped

1–1½ fresh hot green chillies

1 teaspoon very finely grated, peeled fresh ginger

1 teaspoon salt

½–1 teaspoon sugar (preferably brown sugar)

Drop the tomatoes into a pot of rapidly boiling water for 10–15 seconds. Drain, rinse under cold water and peel. Core the tomatoes and cut them into large chunks – roughly 1 inch (2.5cm) cubes.

Heat the oil in a medium-sized pot over a medium flame. When hot, put in the cumin seeds. A few seconds later, put in the garlic. Let the garlic pieces turn a medium-brown colour. Now put in the onion and green chillies. Stir and sauté for about 2 minutes. Now put in the tomatoes, ginger, salt, and sugar. Bring to a boil. Cover, leaving the lid slightly ajar, turn heat to low, and simmer for about 10 minutes or until tomatoes are just tender.

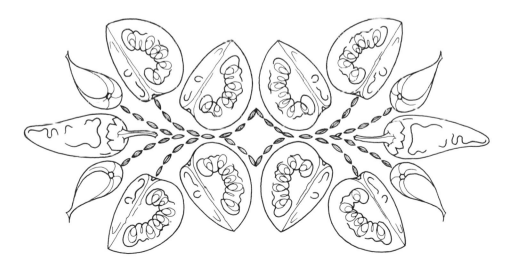

Turnips with fresh coriander and mint

Rasedar shaljum

I have always had a fondness for turnips. The same, however, was not true for my three children, until I finally won them over with this dish.

You could serve turnips with 'Lamb with onions' (page 46) and rice or an Indian bread.

Serves 6:

2 lb (1kg) turnips (weight without leaves)
4 tablespoons vegetable oil
12 oz (375g) fresh tomatoes, peeled (see page 29) or tinned tomatoes may be substituted
A 1 inch (2.5cm) cube of ginger, peeled and grated to a pulp
1 tablespoon ground coriander seeds
$\frac{1}{2}$ teaspoon ground turmeric
$\frac{1}{4}$–$\frac{1}{2}$ teaspoon cayenne pepper
$\frac{3}{4}$ pint (425ml) water
3 tablespoons very finely chopped fresh coriander
2 tablespoons very finely chopped fresh mint
$1\frac{1}{2}$ teaspoons salt

Peel the turnips and cut them in half, lengthwise. Put the cut ends flat against your chopping board and cut them, lengthwise, into $\frac{1}{3}$ inch (1cm) thick slices.

Heat the oil in a fairly wide pot over a medium-high flame. When hot, put in the tomatoes. Stir and fry for about 2 minutes. Add the ginger, coriander, turmeric, and cayenne. Stir and fry another 2 minutes or until the sauce is thick and paste like. Add the turnips, $\frac{3}{4}$ pint (425ml) water, fresh coriander, mint, and salt. Cover, leaving the lid very slightly ajar, and cook on medium-low heat for 20 minutes. Stir a few times as the turnips cook. Now cover the pot tightly and cook on low heat another 10 minutes or until turnips are tender. You should have a little thick sauce left at the bottom of your pot which can be served spooned over the turnips.

PULSES

Pulses – dried beans, split peas, and lentils – are a staple in India and help provide a large measure of the daily protein for families who eat meat rarely or are vegetarian.

But beans, by themselves, are an incomplete food and need to be complemented – at the same meal – with a grain (rice or bread) and a dairy product (such as yoghurt or cheese). When nutritionists tell us today that this food combination has as much protein as a steak, I cannot help but think of the villagers in India whose basic diet, for centuries, has been *dals* (split peas) and rice or bread, washed down with a glass of buttermilk. Perhaps these villagers are not so badly off, after all!

Apart from their food value, I find beans very versatile. Their non-assertive tastes and textures allow them to be used easily in soups. They also combine beautifully with meats and vegetables to make excellent main courses.

Sometimes pulses can be hard to digest. The same Indian forbears who worked out that a nutritionally balanced vegetarian meal contained pulses, grains, and dairy products, also knew – I do not know how – that certain seasonings made beans more digestible. Today pulses in India are almost always cooked with at least one of the following: ginger, asafetida, and turmeric.

We have many different types of pulses in India. Some are left whole, others are split and sometimes skinned. It is the split peas that are called *dals*. The splitting helps to cook them much faster.

All pulses need to be picked over and washed as the packets often include small stones and husks. Whole beans should either be soaked in water overnight before they are cooked or else they can be boiled in water for 2 minutes and then left to soak in the boiling water for an hour. The cooking time for all pulses varies according to their freshness. The fresher they are, the faster they cook. When cooking split peas, Indians always leave the lid slightly ajar. The reason for this is that split peas create a lot of thick froth as they cook and this blocks up the normal escape routes for the steam. So the pot boils over, creating a mess on the cooker. Leaving the lid slightly ajar helps to avoid this.

All beans should be stored in tightly lidded containers.
Here is a description of the pulses I have used in this book:

Red split lentils
Masoor dal

These salmon-coloured, round, split lentils are available widely in most supermarkets. They turn pale yellow during cooking and have a pleasant, mild flavour.

Whole green lentils

These round, flying-saucer-shaped, greenish-brown lentils are very similar to our unsplit, unskinned *masoor*. They are available in all supermarkets and have the virtue of cooking quite fast.

Moong dal

This is the skinned and split version of the same mung bean that is used to make bean sprouts for oriental cooking. The grains are pale yellow and somewhat elongated. This is, perhaps, the most popular North Indian *dal*. It has a mild, aristocratic flavour and is sold by Indian, Pakistani and Greek grocers, and increasingly by many supermarkets.

Chana dal

This is very similar to the yellow split peas that are sold in supermarkets, only the grains are smaller and the flavour 'meatier' and sweeter. *Chana dal* is sold mainly by Indian and Pakistani grocers. Yellow split peas may be substituted for *chana dal* in my recipes.

Black-eyed beans
Lobhia

These excellent beans, greyish or beige ovals, graced with a dark dot, are sold widely in all supermarkets. They have a slightly smokey flavour.

Chickpeas
Chhole

This large, heart-shaped, beige-coloured pea is sold by most supermarkets as well as South Asian, and Middle Eastern grocers. It lends itself to being cooked as a spicy snack food as well as being combined with meats and vegetables.

Red kidney beans
Rajma

These large, dark-red, kidney-shaped beans are available in all supermarkets as well as Asian groceries.

Aduki beans
Ma

These smaller red beans look like the children of red kidney beans. For some reason, they are sold by their Japanese name, *aduki*, in most health food stores and supermarkets.

Red split lentils with cumin seed
Masoor dal

This salmon coloured split pea turns dull yellow when cooked. It is sold as 'Egyptian lentils' in some Middle Eastern stores. It is best served with a rice dish and almost any Indian meat and vegetable you like.

Serves 4–6:

7 oz (200g) red split lentils (masoor dal), picked over, washed and drained

$1\frac{3}{4}$ pints (1 litre) water

2 thin slices of unpeeled ginger

$\frac{1}{2}$ teaspoon ground turmeric

1 teaspoon salt, or to taste

3 tablespoons ghee or vegetable oil

A pinch of ground asafetida, optional

1 teaspoon whole cumin seeds

1 teaspoon ground coriander seeds

$\frac{1}{4}$ teaspoon cayenne pepper

2 tablespoons finely chopped fresh coriander

Combine the lentils and $1\frac{3}{4}$ pints (1 litre) water in a heavy pot. Bring to a simmer. Remove any scum that collects at the top. Add the ginger and turmeric. Stir to mix. Cover, leaving the lid very slightly ajar, turn heat to low, and simmer gently for $1\frac{1}{2}$ hours or until lentils are tender. Stir every 5 minutes during the last half hour to prevent sticking. Add the salt and stir to mix. Remove ginger slices.

Heat the *ghee* in a small frying pan over a medium flame. When hot, put in the asafetida. A second later, put in the cumin seeds. Let the seeds sizzle for a few seconds. Now put in the ground coriander and cayenne. Stir once and then quickly pour the contents of the pan, *ghee* and spices, into the pot with the lentils. Stir to mix.

Sprinkle the fresh coriander over the top when you serve.

Red split lentils with cabbage

Masoor dal aur band gobi

I often eat this with rice and 'Lemony chicken with fresh coriander' (page 73).

Serves 4–6:

7 oz (200g) red split lentils, picked over, washed, and drained

2 pints (1.15 litres) water

$\frac{1}{2}$ teaspoon ground turmeric

5 tablespoons vegetable oil

1 teaspoon whole cumin seeds

2–4 cloves garlic, peeled and finely chopped

3 oz (75g) onion, peeled and cut into fine slices

$\frac{1}{2}$ lb (225g) cored and finely shredded cabbage

1–2 fresh hot green chillies, finely sliced

1$\frac{1}{2}$ teaspoons salt

4 oz (110g) tomato, peeled (see page 29) and finely chopped

$\frac{1}{2}$ teaspoon peeled and finely grated fresh ginger

Put the lentils and 2 pints (1.15 litres) water into a heavy pot and bring to a boil. Remove any scum that collects at the top. Add the turmeric and stir to mix. Cover, leaving the lid very slightly ajar, turn heat down to low, and simmer gently for 1 hour and 15 minutes. Stir a few times during the last half hour.

While the lentils cook, heat the oil in an 8–9 inch (20–23cm) frying pan over a medium flame. When hot, put in the cumin seeds. Let them sizzle for 3–4 seconds. Now put in the garlic. As soon as the garlic pieces begin to brown, put in the onion, cabbage, and green chillies. Stir and fry the cabbage mixture for about 10 minutes or until it begins to brown and turn slightly crisp. Add $\frac{1}{4}$ teaspoon salt to this mixture and stir it in. Turn off the heat under the frying pan.

When the lentils have cooked for 1 hour and 15 minutes, add 1$\frac{1}{4}$ teaspoon salt, the tomato, and ginger to the pot. Stir to mix. Cover and cook another 10 minutes. Add the cabbage mixture and any remaining oil in the frying pan. Stir to mix and bring to a simmer. Simmer, uncovered, 2–3 minutes or until cabbage is heated through.

Whole green lentils with garlic and onion

This is a very simple – and flavourful – method of cooking the humble lentil. You could serve them with 'Goan-style sweet and sour pork' (page 59) or any other meat dish, 'Simple buttery rice with onion' (page 149) and 'Gujerati green beans' (page 165).

Serve 4–6:

4 tablespoons vegetable oil

½ teaspoon whole cumin seeds

4 cloves garlic, peeled and finely chopped

3 oz (75g) onion, peeled and chopped

7 oz (200g) whole green lentils, washed and drained

1¼ pints (720ml) water

1 teaspoon salt

⅛–¼ teaspoon cayenne pepper

Heat the oil in a heavy pot over a medium flame. When hot, put in the cumin seeds. A few seconds later, put in the garlic. Stir and fry until the garlic pieces turn a medium brown colour. Now put in the onion. Stir and fry until the onion pieces begin to turn brown at the edges. Put in the lentils and the water. Bring to a boil. Cover, turn heat to low and simmer for about an hour or until lentils are tender. Add the salt and the cayenne. Stir to mix and simmer gently for another 5 minutes.

Whole green lentils with spinach and ginger

This very nourishing dish goes well with 'Beef baked with yoghurt and black pepper' (page 50) and 'Lamb with onions' (page 46).

Serves 6:

7 oz (200g) whole green lentils, picked over, washed, and drained

1¼ pints(720ml) water

6 tablespoons vegetable oil

1–2 fresh, hot green chillies, finely sliced

1 teaspoon very finely grated fresh ginger

8 well-packed tablespoons chopped fresh coriander

1¼ lb (560g) fresh spinach, trimmed, washed and chopped

2 teaspoons salt

Freshly ground black pepper

2 tablespoons lemon juice – or more, according to taste

Put the lentils and the water into a heavy pot and bring to a boil. Cover, turn heat to low and simmer gently for 1 hour.

Over a medium flame, heat the oil in a pot large enough to hold the spinach. When hot, put in the chillies and the ginger. Stir and fry for 10 seconds. Add the fresh coriander and spinach. Stir and cook until the spinach has wilted. Now put in the cooked lentils and the salt. Stir to mix and bring to a simmer. Cover and cook very gently for 25 minutes. Add the black pepper and lemon juice, stir to mix, and cook uncovered for another 5 minutes. Check seasonings.

Dry moong dal

Sookhi moong dal

Not all *dals* are cooked to be thin and soupy. Here the grains stand out, all plump and separate, and the *dal* has a fairly dry look. It is usually not eaten with rice but with breads and other meats and vegetables. I love to sprinkle some crisp, browned onions over the top, just before I serve it. You will find a recipe for the onions on page 174.

Serves 4–6:

7 oz (200g) moong dal

1 teaspoon ground coriander seeds

1 teaspoon ground cumin seeds

$\frac{1}{4}$ teaspoon ground turmeric

$\frac{1}{8}$–$\frac{1}{4}$ teaspoon cayenne pepper

1 tablespoon plus 8 fl oz (225ml) water

2 tablespoons vegetable oil

About $\frac{1}{2}$ teaspoon salt

2 tablespoons ghee (see page 25)

$\frac{1}{2}$ teaspoon whole cumin seeds

1 whole, hot dried red chilli, optional

Pick over the *dal* and wash it in several changes of water. Drain. Put the *dal* in a bowl. Pour about $1\frac{1}{2}$ pints (850ml) of water over it and let it soak for 3 hours. Drain.

Combine the ground coriander, ground cumin, turmeric, and 1 tablespoon of water in a small cup.

Heat the oil in a heavy pot over a medium flame. When it is hot, put in the spice mixture from the cup and stir once. Quickly put in the drained *dal*. Stir to mix. Add the salt and 8 fl oz (225ml) of water. Bring to a boil. Cover tightly, turn heat to very low, and cook for 15 minutes. The *dal* grains should now be quite tender.

Just before you sit down to eat, put the hot *dal* into a serving bowl. Heat the *ghee* in a small pot or a small frying pan. When it is very hot, put in the whole cumin seeds. Let them sizzle for a few seconds. Now put in the whole chilli and stir it about for 2–3 seconds – it should puff up and darken. Now pour the *ghee* and spices over the cooked *dal*. You may stir to mix or else leave the spices on the top as a kind of garnish.

If you decide to use the fried onions, you may sprinkle these over the *dal* at the last minute as well.

(Those unfamiliar with Indian foods should be warned that the whole chilli is very hot and not meant to be eaten – except by those who know what they are doing.)

Small yellow split peas
Chana dal

Of all the *dals*, this one perhaps has the 'meatiest' taste. At its best, it also has a gentle sweetness. *Chana dal* is sold only by Indian grocers. If you cannot find it, substitute yellow split peas. You could serve this *dal* with rice, 'Chicken with tomatoes' (page 75) and 'Cauliflower and potatoes' (page 109).

Serves 4–6:

8 oz (225g) chana dal or yellow split peas, picked over, washed, and drained

2 pints (1.15 litres) water

½ teaspoon ground turmeric

2 thin slices of unpeeled ginger

¾–1 teaspoon salt

¼ teaspoon garam masala (see page 18)

3 tablespoons ghee or vegetable oil (see page 25)

½ teaspoon whole cumin seeds

1–2 cloves garlic, peeled and chopped

¼–½ teaspoon red chilli powder

Put the *dal* in a heavy pot along with 2 pints (1.5 litres) water. Bring to a boil and remove any surface scum. Add the turmeric and ginger. Cover, leaving the lid just very slightly ajar, turn heat to low, and simmer gently for 1½ hours or until the *dal* is tender. Stir every 5 minutes or so during the last half hour of cooking to prevent sticking. Add the salt and *garam masala* to the *dal*. Stir to mix.

Heat the *ghee* in a small frying pan over a medium flame. When hot, put in the cumin seeds. A couple of seconds later, put in the garlic. Stir and fry until the garlic pieces are lightly browned. Put the chilli powder into the pan. Immediately, lift the pan off the heat and pour its entire contents – *ghee* and spices – into the pot with the dal. Stir to mix.

Black-eyed beans with mushrooms

Lobhia aur khumbi

I like this bean dish so much, I often find myself eating it up with a spoon, all by itself. At a meal, I serve it with *Rogan josh* ('Red lamb or beef stew', page 51) or with 'Chicken in a fried onion sauce' (page 72). Rice or Indian breads should be served on the side.

Serves 6:

½ lb (225g) dried black-eyed beans, picked over, washed, and drained

2 pints (1.15 litres) water

½ lb (225g) fresh mushrooms

6 tablespoons vegetable oil

1 teaspoon whole cumin seeds

A 1 inch (2.5cm) stick of cinnamon

5 oz (150g) onions, peeled and chopped

4 cloves garlic, peeled and very finely chopped

14 oz (400g) tomatoes, peeled (see page 29) and chopped

2 teaspoons ground coriander seeds

1 teaspoon ground cumin seeds

½ teaspoon ground turmeric

¼ teaspoon cayenne pepper

2 teaspoons salt

Freshly ground black pepper

3 tablespoons chopped fresh coriander (fresh parsley may be substituted)

Put the beans and water into a heavy pot and bring to a boil. Cover, turn heat to low and simmer gently for 2 minutes. Turn off the heat and let the pot sit, covered and undisturbed, for 1 hour.

While the pot is resting, cut the mushrooms through their stems into ⅛ inch (3mm) thick slices.

Heat the oil in a frying pan over a medium-high flame. When hot, put in the whole cumin seeds and the cinnamon stick. Let them sizzle for 5–6 seconds. Now put in the onions and garlic. Stir and fry until the onion pieces turn brown at the edges. Put in the mushrooms. Stir and fry until the mushrooms wilt. Now put in the tomatoes, ground coriander, ground cumin, turmeric, and cayenne. Stir and cook for a minute. Cover, turn heat to low and let this mixture cook in its own juices for 10 minutes. Turn off the heat under the frying pan.

Bring the beans to a boil again. Cover, turn heat to low and simmer for 20–30 minutes or until beans are tender. To this bean and water mixture, add the mushroom mixture, salt, black pepper, and fresh coriander. Stir to mix and bring to a simmer. Simmer, uncovered, on medium-low heat for another 30 minutes. Stir occasionally. Remove cinnamon stick before serving.

Sour chickpeas

Khatte chhole

Known variously as chickpeas, garbanzos, and in India, *chholas* and *kabuli chanas*, this unsplit, heart-shaped legume provides North Indians with some of their tastiest snack foods. As a child in Delhi, I much preferred buying my *chholas* from itinerant street vendors. They were invariably sourer, spicier and much tastier than anything produced at home. (One of the reasons for my partiality to 'unclean bazaar food', as my father called it, may well have been that we were forbidden to eat it!) In this recipe, I have tried to reproduce that elusive 'bazaar' taste which made me an addict of the dish many years ago.

Although *Khatte chhole* are generally eaten as a snack in India, I serve them at my lunches and dinners, with vegetables, meats and rice.

Serves 6:

$\frac{3}{4}$ lb (350g) chickpeas picked over, washed and drained

3 pints (1.75 litres) water

10 11 oz (275–300g) onions, peeled and very finely chopped

About $2\frac{1}{2}$ teaspoons salt

1 fresh, hot green chilli, finely chopped

1 tablespoon very finely grated fresh ginger (grate after peeling)

4 tablespoons lemon juice

6 tablespoons vegetable oil

$\frac{1}{2}$ lb (225g) tomatoes, finely chopped

1 tablespoon ground coriander seeds

1 tablespoon ground cumin seeds

$\frac{1}{2}$ teaspoon ground turmeric

2 teaspoons garam masala (see page 18)

$\frac{1}{4}$ teaspoon cayenne pepper

Soak the chickpeas in 3 pints (1.75 litres) of water for 20 hours. Put the chickpeas and their soaking liquid into a large pot and bring to a boil. Cover, lower heat and simmer gently for an hour and a half or until chickpeas are tender. Strain the chickpeas and save the cooking liquid.

Put 2 tablespoons of the chopped onions, $\frac{1}{2}$ teaspoon salt, green chilli, ginger and lemon juice into a tea-cup. Mix well and set aside.

Heat the oil in a heavy, wide, casserole-type pot over a medium-high flame. When hot, put in the remaining chopped onions. Stir and fry for 8–10 minutes or until the onion bits develop reddish-brown spots. Add the tomatoes. Continue to stir and fry another 5–6 minutes, mashing the tomato pieces with the back of a slotted spoon. Put in the coriander, cumin and turmeric. Stir and cook for about 30 seconds. Now put in the drained chickpeas, 14 fl oz (400ml) of their cooking liquid, 2 teaspoons of salt, the *garam masala* and cayenne. Stir to mix and bring to a simmer. Cover, turn heat to low and cook very gently for 20 minutes. Stir a few times during this period. Add the mixture in the tea-cup. Stir again to mix. Serve hot or lukewarm.

Red kidney beans

Punjabi rajma

Rajma, red kidney beans, are cooked slowly in Punjabi villages, often in the ashes of a *tandoor* or clay oven. I used to cook them for $4\frac{1}{2}$ hours on top of the stove but have now found a much quicker method. This dish may also be made with aduki beans or an equal mixture of red kidney beans and aduki beans. These beans may be served with *Rogan josh* ('Red lamb or beef stew', page 51) and an Indian bread.

Serves 4–6:

6 oz (175g) red kidney beans picked over, washed, and drained

$2\frac{1}{4}$ pints (1.25 litres) water

3 thin slices of unpeeled ginger plus half teaspoon of peeled and very finely chopped ginger

About 1 teaspoon salt

$1\frac{1}{2}$ tablespoons lemon juice

$\frac{1}{4}$ teaspoon garam masala (see page 18)

5 fl oz (150ml) double cream

3 tablespoons ghee (see page 25) or vegetable oil

$\frac{1}{2}$ teaspoon whole cumin seeds

1 clove garlic, peeled and finely chopped

2 whole, dried hot red chillies

Put the beans and water into a heavy pot and bring to a boil. Turn heat to low and simmer for 2 minutes. Turn off the heat and let the beans sit, uncovered, for 1 hour. Add the 3 slices of ginger to the beans and bring them to a boil again. Fast boil for 10 minutes, then cover, leaving the lid very slightly ajar. Turn heat to low, and simmer gently for 1 hour. Discard the ginger slices.

You may now mash the beans against the sides of the pot or take half the beans and their liquid and purée them in a blender. Pour this puréed paste back into the pot of beans. This gives the dish a pleasant texture. Add the salt, lemon juice, *garam masala*, and cream. Stir to mix and check seasonings.

Heat the *ghee* in a small frying pan over a medium flame. When hot, put in the cumin seeds. Two seconds later, put in the finely chopped garlic and the remaining chopped ginger. Stir and fry until the garlic browns lightly. Put in the red chillies. Stir them once and then pour the contents of the pan, *ghee* and seasonings, into the pot with the beans. Stir to mix.

N.B. The whole red chillies are not meant to be eaten.

BREADS

Thee are all kinds of breads in India, most of them unleavened, eaten in the North at every single meal. Many of these everyday breads are made with a *very* finely ground wholewheat flour that we call *ata*. I find that the British flour that approximates *ata* best is wheatmeal flour because it has just enough bran in it to give it body without making it too coarse for our soft, pliable breads. Of course, if you have access to Indian grocers and can buy *ata* (sometimes called chapati flour) do, by all means, use it.

Some of our breads, such as the *poori*, are deep-fried. The ideal utensil for this is the Indian *karhai* because it is very economical on oil and because it prevents hot oil from splashing on to the cooker. A deep frying pan may be used as a substitute.

Many other breads are cooked on a *tava*, a concave cast iron plate that is heated before breads such as *chapatis* and *parathas* are slapped on to it. As I have suggested in the chapter on equipment, a cast-iron frying pan makes a perfectly adequate substitute.

You will find one other kind of bread in this chapter. It is really a savoury pancake and is made, not with flour but with a split pea (*moong dal*) batter. Such pancakes are a very common breakfast and snack food in India, specially in the West and South.

OPPOSITE PAGE:
Poppadums, *Paapar* (page 180)
Deep-fried, stuffed, savoury pastries, *Samosas* (page 187)
Beetroot with onions, *Shorvedar chukander* (page 104)
Dry moong dal, *Sookhi moong dal* (page 126)

OVERLEAF:
Yoghurt with walnuts and fresh coriander, *Akhrote ka raita* (page 163)
Spicy cucumber wedges, *Kheere ke tukray* (page 172)
Leavened oven bread, *Naan* (page 139)
Tandoori style chicken, *Tandoori murghi* (page 66)

Deep-fried, puffy bread

Poori

Pooris look like puffed-up balloons. They are crispy-soft, delicious, and may be eaten with almost all Indian meats, vegetables, and pulses. They are also easy to make. Rolled out discs of dough are put into hot oil – the oil *must* be hot or the *pooris* will not 'blister' and puff – and they cook magically in just a few seconds.

As *pooris* are best eaten hot, I have taught my entire family how to make them. I make three *pooris* per person. Then, if anyone wants more, they are told to go into the kitchen and make their own. And they do! Our *poori* dinners invariably turn into a 'happening' with flour-covered children and husband wandering in and out of the kitchen, rolling pin in hand and a look of great achievement on their faces.

A word of caution: As the cooking oil for *pooris* is hot, care should be taken not to splash it around. An Indian *kurhai* is the safest and most economical utensil for deep-frying. If you do not have one, use a *deep* frying pan. Do not drop the *poori* into the oil from a great height or it will splash. Bring your hand as close to the surface of the oil and lay the *poori* over it. Oil has no steam and will not burn you unless you touch it. When turning the *poori* over, bring it first to the edge of your utensil and then use the edge to help you turn it over. This, again, is to avoid splashes. Drain the cooked *poori* over the oil for a second or two before putting it in a platter. If you take these simple precautions (necessary for any deep-frying), *poori*-making can be fun.

Makes 12 pooris and serves 4

4 oz (110g) sieved wheatmeal flour

4 oz (110g) plain flour

½ teaspoon salt

2 tablespoons vegetable oil plus more for deep-frying

3½ fl oz (100ml) water

Put the two flours and salt in a bowl. Dribble the 2 tablespoons oil over the top. Rub the oil in with your fingers so the mixture resembles coarse breadcrumbs. Slowly add the water to form a stiff ball of dough. Empty the ball on to a clean work surface. Knead it for 10–12 minutes or until it is smooth. Form a ball. Rub about ¼ teaspoon oil on the ball and slip it into a polythene bag. Set it aside for 30 minutes.

Knead the dough again, and divide it into 12 equal balls. Keep 11 of them covered while you work with the twelfth. Flatten this ball and roll it out into a 5–5½ inch (13–14cm) round. If you have the space, roll out all the *pooris* and keep them in a single layer, covered with cling film.

Over a medium flame, set about 1 inch

(2.5cm) of oil to heat in a small, deep frying pan. Let it get very, very hot. Meanwhile, line a platter with kitchen paper. Lift up one *poori* and lay it carefully over the surface of the hot oil. It might sink to the bottom but it should rise in seconds and begin to sizzle. Using the back of a slotted spoon, push the *poori* gently into the oil with tiny, *swift* strokes. Within seconds, the *poori* will puff up. Turn it over and cook the second side for about 10 seconds. Remove it with a slotted spoon and put it on the platter. Make all the *pooris* this way. The first layer on the platter may be covered with a layer of kitchen paper. More *pooris* can then be spread over the top. Serve the *pooris* hot.

Flat bread

Chapati

Sometimes small and delicate and at other times large and thick, this is the basic, flat and disc-like, Indian bread eaten over most of north India. It is made out of a very finely ground whole-wheat flour that is sold in Indian shops as *ata* or 'chapati flour'. I find that finely sifted wheatmeal flour makes an adequate substitute. If you are using the wheatmeal flour, make sure you sift it before you weigh it. Some people like to add a little bit of salt to the flour. This should be done before you make the dough.

Chapati dough has to be quite soft. The amount of water you use to form it will vary with the type of flour and the general humidity in the air. Use the quantity of water I have suggested as a guideline but don't be afraid to use more or less as you see fit. Because the dough is soft, *chapatis* are rolled out into their round, disc shape with the assistance of a fair amount of extra flour.

Chapatis are traditionally cooked on a *tava*, a slightly concave, circular, cast iron plate, which is left to heat by itself before the first *chapati* is slapped on to it. This preheating prevents the *chapati* from becoming hard and brittle. If you don't have a *tava*, you could use a heavy, cast iron frying pan.

First, the *chapati* is cooked briefly on both sides. Then, in India at any rate, it is put directly on top of live charcoal. It is this exposure to intense heat that makes it puff up. Since few of us have live charcoal in our kitchens any more, this same puffing-up process may be done by putting the *chapati* directly on top of a low gas flame. The time a *chapati* spends sitting on the flame is very brief, and, for some reason, it does not burn or catch fire.

You could, if you like, spread a little butter or *ghee* on top of the *chapati* as soon as it is made. Usually, *chapatis* are stacked, one on top of the other, as they are being made, and kept covered with a napkin, so they stay hot. Needless to say, they deflate in the process but still taste wonderful. The only way to eat a puffed-up *chapati* is to eat it as it comes off the cooker.

Perfection in *chapati*-making does come with practice. If your first few *chapatis* turn out a little odd-shaped, remember that they will still taste good.

Chapatis freeze well and defrost easily, without losing taste or texture.

Makes about 15

9 oz (250g) sieved wheatmeal flour plus extra for dusting

6 fl oz (175ml) water

Put the 9 oz (250g) flour in a bowl. Slowly add about 6 fl oz (175ml) water, gathering the flour together as you do so, to form a soft dough. Knead the dough for 6–8 minutes or until it is smooth. Put the dough in a bowl. Cover with a damp cloth and leave for half an hour.

Set an Indian *tava* or any other cast iron frying pan to heat over a medium-low flame for 10 minutes. When it is very hot, turn the heat to low.

Knead the dough again and divide it, roughly, into 15 parts. It will be fairly sticky, so rub your hands with a little flour when handling it.

Take one part of the dough and form a ball. Flour your work surface generously and roll the ball in it. Press down on the ball to make a patty. Now roll this patty out, dusting it very frequently with flour, until it is about $5\frac{1}{2}$ inches (14cm) in diameter. Pick up this *chapati* and pat it between your hands to shake off extra flour and then slap it on to the hot *tava* or frying pan. Let it cook on low heat for about a minute. Its underside should develop white spots. Turn the *chapati* over (I use my hands to do this but you could use a pair of tongs) and cook for about half a minute on the second side. Take the pan off the stove and put the *chapati* directly on top of the low flame. It should puff up in seconds.

Turn the *chapati* over and let the second side sit on the flame for a few seconds. Put the *chapati* in a deep plate lined with a large napkin. Fold the napkin over the *chapati*. Make all *chapatis* this way.

Ideally, *chapatis* should be eaten as soon as they are made. But if you wish to eat them later, wrap the whole stack in aluminium foil and either refrigerate for a day or freeze. The *chapatis* may be reheated, still wrapped in foil, in a gas mark 7, 425°F (220°C) oven for 15–20 minutes.

Layered bread

Paratha

These are the triangular breads that we eat frequently with our meals and even pack up as school lunches for our children. With them, we have vegetables such as 'Spicy green beans' (page 103) or 'Aubergines cooked in the pickling style' (page 100) and meats such as 'Chicken with cream' (page 74).

Makes 12 and should serve 4–6:

6 oz (175g) sieved wheatmeal flour

6½ oz (190g) plain flour plus some extra for dusting

½ teaspoon salt

About 10 tablespoons vegetable oil (or melted ghee)

7 fl oz (200ml) water

Put the two flours and salt in a bowl. Dribble 2 tablespoons of the oil over the top. Rub the oil in with your fingertips until the mixture resembles coarse breadcrumbs. Slowly add about anywhere from 5 to 7 fl oz (150–200ml) water and gather the flour together to form a softish ball.

Empty the ball on to a clean work surface. Knead for about 10 minutes or until you have a smooth, soft, but not sticky dough. Form a ball. Rub the ball with about ¼ teaspoon oil and slip it into a polythene bag for 30 minutes or longer.

Set a large, cast iron frying pan to heat on a medium-low flame. Meanwhile, knead the dough again and form 12 equal balls. Keep 11 of them covered while you work with the twelfth. Flatten this ball and dust it with some plain flour. Roll it out, into a 6 inch (15cm) round, dusting your work surface with flour whenever necessary. Spread ¼ teaspoon oil over the surface of the *paratha* and fold it in half. Spread about $\frac{1}{8}$ teaspoon oil over the surface of the half that is on top and fold it into half again to form a triangle. Roll out this triangle into a larger triangle with 7 inch (18cm) sides. Dust with flour whenever necessary.

Brush the hot frying pan with $\frac{1}{4}$ teaspoon oil and slap the *paratha* on to it. Let the *paratha* cook for a minute. Now brush the top generously with 1 teaspoon oil. The brushing will take about 30 seconds. Turn the *paratha* over and cook the second side for a minute or so. Both sides should have reddish-gold spots. Move the *paratha* around as you cook so all ends are exposed evenly to the heat.

Put the cooked *paratha* in a plate. Cover either with an inverted plate or with a piece of aluminium foil. Make all *parathas* this way.

If *parathas* are not to be eaten right away, wrap them tightly in aluminium foil. The whole, wrapped bundle of *parathas* may then be heated in a gas mark 6, 400°F (200°C) oven for 15–20 minutes.

Leavened oven bread

Naan

Naans and other similar flat leavened breads are eaten all the way from the Caucasus down through north-western India. In India, the baking is done in very hot clay ovens or *tandoors*. The breads are slapped on to the inside walls and cook quite happily alongside skewered chickens. At home, where most of us do not have *tandoors*, *naans* can be baked by using both the oven and the grill.

Naans may be cooked both with and without egg. If you decide not to use the egg, just increase the yoghurt by about 4 tablespoons.

Naans may be eaten with almost any Indian meat or vegetable.

Makes 6 large breads:

¼ pint (150ml) hand-hot milk

2 teaspoons castor sugar

2 teaspoons dried active yeast

1 lb (450g) plain flour

½ teaspoon salt

1 teaspoon baking powder

2 tablespoons vegetable oil plus a little extra

5 fl oz (150ml) plain yoghurt, lightly beaten

1 large egg, lightly beaten

Put the milk in a bowl. Add 1 teaspoon of the sugar and the yeast. Stir to mix. Set aside for 15–20 minutes or until the yeast has dissolved and the mixture is frothy.

Sift the flour, salt, and baking powder into a large bowl. Add the remaining 1 teaspoon sugar, the yeast mixture, the 2 tablespoons vegetable oil, the yoghurt, and the egg. Mix and form a ball of dough.

Empty the ball of dough on to a clean work surface and knead it for 10 minutes or more, until it is smooth and satiny. Form into a ball. Pour about ¼ teaspoon oil into a large bowl and roll the ball of dough in it. Cover the bowl with a piece of cling film and set aside in a warm, draught-free place for 1 hour or until the dough has doubled in bulk.

Preheat your oven to the highest temperature. Put the heaviest baking tray you own to heat in the oven. Preheat your grill.

Punch down the dough and knead it again. Divide it into 6 equal balls. Keep five of them covered while you work with the sixth. Roll this ball into a tear-shaped *naan*, about 10 inches (25.5cm) in length and about 5 inches (13cm) at its widest. Remove the hot baking tray from the oven and slap the *naan* on to it. Put it immediately into the oven for 3 minutes. It should puff up. Now place the baking tray and *naan* under the grill, about 3–4 inches (7.5–10cm) away from the heat, for about 30 seconds or until the top of the *naan* browns slightly. Wrap the *naan* in a clean tea towel. Make all the *naans* this way and serve hot.

Moong dal pancakes with peas

Gujerati poore

Savoury pancakes made out of split peas, or rice and split peas, provide much of India with a nourishing snack food. These protein-rich pancakes are also eaten by many vegetarian Indians at breakfast, usually accompanied by a chutney and a glass of fresh buttermilk. You could also serve them with tea.

Makes about 9:

$6\frac{1}{2}$ oz (190g) moong dal, picked over, washed, and drained

2 oz (50g) shelled peas

A 1 inch (2.5cm) cube of ginger, peeled and coarsely chopped

2–3 cloves garlic, peeled

1–2 fresh, hot green chillies, cut into 4 pieces each

1 teaspoon salt

$\frac{1}{4}$ teaspoon ground turmeric

3 fl oz (75ml) plus 1 tablespoon water

2 oz (50g) onion, peeled and minced

2 tablespoons finely chopped coriander

$\frac{1}{4}$ teaspoon baking soda

About 4 fl oz (125ml) vegetable oil

Put the *dal* in a bowl. Add $1\frac{3}{4}$ pints (1 litre) water and soak for 5 hours. Drain.

Drop the peas into boiling water for 3–4 minutes or until they are tender. Drain and chop coarsely.

Combine the ginger, garlic, chillies, salt, turmeric, *dal*, and 3 fl oz (75ml) plus 1 tablespoon water in the container of an electric blender. Blend until you have a smooth batter. Let the machine run for 2–3 minutes more so the batter gets light and airy.

Empty the batter into a bowl. Add the onion and fresh coriander and peas. Mix. The batter may now be covered and refrigerated, if you like, for up to 24 hours.

Just before you get ready to cook, add the baking soda and mix it in. Remember to stir the batter before you make each pancake.

Brush an 8 inch (20cm) non-stick frying pan with about 1 teaspoon of oil and set it to heat over a medium-low flame. Remove about 2 fl oz (55ml) of batter. When the oil is hot, drop this batter right in the centre of the pan. Now, place the rounded bottom of a soup spoon on the centre of the blob of batter. Using a gentle but continuous spiral motion, spread the batter outwards with the back of the spoon, smoothing out any ridges along the way. Make a pancake that is about $5\frac{1}{2}$–6 inches (14–15cm) in diameter. Dribble a teaspoon of oil over the pancake and another $\frac{1}{2}$ teaspoon around its edges. Cover the pan and let the pancake cook for 2 minutes or until its underside turns a reddish colour. Uncover the pan and turn the pancake over. Cook the pancake on the second side for $1\frac{1}{2}$ minutes or until it develops small red spots. Remove the pancake and put it on a plate. Cover with a second plate, inverted over the first. Make all the pancakes this way, making sure you stir the batter each time.

These pancakes are best eaten hot, just as soon as they are made. You could, if you wish, stack them on a sheet of aluminium foil and then wrap them into a bundle. The whole bundle can be heated in an oven at gas mark 7, 425°F (220°C) for 15 minutes.

RICE

My English friends are always telling me that they cannot cook rice. They can hardly be blamed for their phobia. It starts, I think, with inadequate – inaccurate, in fact – instructions on rice packages that invariably suggest using far more water than rice really requires. The rice ends up by being mushy and the people who are cooking it often think that it is their fault. It is not.

There are, actually, many methods of cooking rice well. You will find several in the chapter that follows. Rice can be cooked like pasta, in a lot of boiling water until it is half done. Then it can be drained and 'dried off' in a slow oven. Rice can be cooked completely on top of the cooker with just the correct amount of water needed for absorption. Or you can start cooking rice on top of the cooker with just the amount of water needed for absorption and then finish it off in the oven. The method you choose depends upon the recipe and what you want the rice to do.

If you are unsure about cooking rice, just follow my recipes carefully and you should not go wrong.

There are a few things that are worth remembering when cooking rice:

1   Use a heavy pot with a very tight-fitting lid. If you have a tin-lined copper pot hanging decoratively in your kitchen, this is your chance to use it. An enamelled, cast-iron pot is also good for rice. I find that such pots generally have fairly loose-fitting lids. There is a very quick remedy for this. Just cover the pot tightly with a sheet of aluminium foil first and then with its own lid. You can also make good rice in heavy, stainless steel pots. Any time you are unsure about the fitting of the lid, interpose a layer of aluminium foil between it and the pot. Be sure to crinkle the edges of the foil so that hardly any steam escapes. In many of my recipes, the rice ends up by cooking in steam. If too much of it escapes, the rice will not cook properly.

2   For best results, rice should be washed in several changes of water and then soaked for about 30 minutes before it is cooked. The washing gets rid of the starchy powder left over from the milling process. The soaking lets each grain absorb water so it sticks less to the next grain while it is cooking.

3   If you are cooking rice with just enough water or stock needed for absorption, what is the correct proportion of liquid to rice? I like to measure my rice in a clear measuring jug and I never use more than $1\frac{1}{2}$ parts liquid to 1 part rice. If I have soaked the rice, my ratio changes to $1\frac{1}{3}$ parts liquid to 1 part rice.

4   Sometimes I sauté my rice before I add liquid to it. This also helps to keep the grains separate. When you sauté rice, do it gently. Some type of rice grains, such as basmati, are very delicate, particularly after they have been soaked. If you sauté too vigorously, the grains break up into small pieces.

5   Once I cover my rice pot with a lid, I like to cook it on a very, very low flame. If you cannot adjust your heat to this very, very low, then use an oven-

proof pot to begin with, cover it tightly as instructed, and pop it into a preheated gas mark 3, 325°F (170°C) oven for 25 minutes.

6   Resist any urge you may have to peep into a covered pot of rice before the cooking time is over. Precious steam will escape and the rice will cook unevenly.

7   If you have a thin layer of rice at the top of your pot that does not get cooked all the way through, while the rest of the rice does, then your lid is not tight enough. Use aluminium foil between the pot and the lid next time around. Meanwhile, salvage your present situation by gently covering the partially cooked rice at the top with some fully cooked rice from the bottom. Add a tablespoon or two of water to the pot, cover tightly, this time using the foil, and cook for another 10 minutes over very low heat.

8   When removing cooked rice from the pot, use a large slotted spoon. Either scrape out the rice gently, layer by layer or else ease the spoon gently into the rice, lift out as much as you can, put it in a platter and then break up any lumps by pressing lightly with the back of the spoon.

I have used two types of rice in this chapter, long grain (which could be labelled 'Patna' or 'American long-grain') and basmati.

Basmati rice grows best in the foothills of the Himalaya Mountains, in both India and Pakistan. Actually, it too is a long grain rice, only the grains are slender, delicate, naturally perfumed, and somewhat more expensive! The best basmati rice is aged for a year before it is sold. This ageing increases its unusual, nutty aroma. While it is not necessary to pick over and wash packaged American rice (though washing will give it a better texture) basmati rice *must* be picked over, washed and soaked before cooking as it often contains small stones and other impurities.

To pick it over, empty the rice onto one end of a large platter. Now work the rice from one side of the platter to the other, inspecting the grains carefully. Push any stones or other suspicious objects to one side.

Washing the grains: put the picked rice in your largest bowl. Now fill the bowl with cold water and gently swirl the rice around in it. The water will become cloudy with starch. Carefully pour the water away, holding back the rice with your free hand. Repeat 5 or 6 times, or as long as it takes for the water to remain reasonably clear.

Soaking: Fill up the bowl again, only this time leave the rice in the water for 20 minutes to half an hour.

Now drain the rice in a sieve. It should sit in the sieve for at least 20 minutes to become fairly dry before you cook it.

If you use this method of preparation, combined with any of the various cooking methods given in the recipes, you will find that you need dramatically less water than you may have come to expect. Also your rice will have light, separated grains and will taste delicious.

The amazing thing about rice is that it can be cooked with almost any spice and combined with any vegetable, pulse, or meat. It is, perhaps, the world's most amenable grain.

Plain, easy-to-cook, rice

Saaday Chaaval

This is the quickest way of cooking American-style, packaged, long-grain rice. It requires no washing and no soaking and may be served with any food.

Serves 4–6

Long-grain rice measured to the 15 fl oz (425ml) level in a glass measuring jug

1 teaspoon salt, optional

½ oz (10g) unsalted butter, optional

1¼ pints (700ml) water

Combine the rice, water, salt and butter in a heavy pot and bring to a boil. Cover very tightly, turn heat to very, very low, and cook, undisturbed, for 25 minutes. Turn off the heat and let the pot rest, still covered and undisturbed, for another 5 minutes.

Plain long-grain rice

Barhiya chaaval

This rice is slightly more elegant than the one in the preceding recipe mainly because it is washed and soaked before being cooked. These steps get rid of the starchy powder on the grains and help them to remain separate and unsplit.

Serves 4–6:

Enough long-grain rice to fill a glass measuring jug to the 15 fl oz (425ml) level

1 teaspoon salt

1 pint (570ml) water

Put the rice in a bowl and wash in several changes of water. Drain. Leave to soak in 2 pints (1.25 litres) of water for 30 minutes. Drain thoroughly.

Put the drained rice, salt and 1 pint (570ml) water in a heavy pot and bring to a boil. Cover with a very tight-fitting lid, turn heat to very, very low and cook for 25 minutes. Take the rice pot off the flame and let it rest, still covered and undisturbed, for another 10 minutes.

South Indian-style light, fluffy rice

Dakshini chaaval

In South India, rice is generally parboiled in a large, round-bottomed, narrow-necked utensil, with lots of water. When it is almost cooked, a cloth is tied to the mouth of the utensil and all the extra water drained out. (This water is later fed to the cows!) The pot is tilted so it lies on its belly over very low heat. A few live coals are placed on top of it as well to dry out the rice grains. Here is how the same rice may be made in a modern kitchen:

Serves 6:

Long-grain rice measured to the 15 fl oz (425ml) level in a glass measuring jug

5 pints (3 litres) water

1 tablespoon salt, optional

1–2 oz (25–50g) unsalted butter, optional

Preheat oven to gas mark 2, 300°F (150°C). Wash the rice in several changes of water and leave it to drain.

Fill a large pot with about 5 pints (3 litres) of water. Add the salt to it if you wish and bring to a rolling boil. Empty the rice into the boiling water in a steady stream, stirring as you do so. Let the water come to a boil again. Boil rapidly for 7 minutes. Drain the rice in a colander. Quickly put the rice in an oven-proof pot. Lay the butter over it, cover tightly and put the pot in the oven for 35 minutes or until rice is done. Mix gently before serving.

Plain basmati rice

Basmati chaaval

I was brought up with this fine-grained rice. Now, as it has become quite expensive, it is only served at festive occasions and at parties.

Serves 6:

Basmati rice measured to the 15 fl oz (425ml) level in a glass measuring jug

1 pint (570ml) water

¾ teaspoon salt

½ oz (10g) unsalted butter

Pick over the rice and put it in a bowl. Wash in several changes of water. Drain. Pour 2 pints (1.25 litres) of fresh water over the rice and let it soak for half an hour. Drain thoroughly.

Combine the rice, salt, butter and 1 pint (570ml) water in a heavy-bottomed pot. Bring to a boil. Cover with a tight-fitting lid, turn heat to very low and cook for 20 minutes. Lift the lid, mix gently but quickly with a fork and cover again. Cook for 5–10 minutes or until tender.

Spiced basmati rice

Masaledar basmati

This is one of the finest – and most delicate – basmati rice dishes. It may be served with an Indian meal or with English dishes such as roast lamb or grilled chicken.

Basmati rice measured to the 15 fl oz (425ml) level in a glass measuring jug

3 tablespoons vegetable oil

2 oz (50g) onion, peeled and finely chopped

$\frac{1}{2}$ a fresh, hot green chilli, finely chopped

$\frac{1}{2}$ teaspoon very finely chopped garlic

$\frac{1}{2}$ teaspoon garam masala (see page 18)

1 teaspoon salt (a bit more if the stock is unsalted)

1 pint (570ml) chicken stock

Pick over the rice and put in a bowl. Wash in several changes of water. Drain. Pour 2 pints (1.25 litres) fresh water over the rice and let it soak for half an hour. Leave to drain in a sieve for 20 minutes.

Heat the oil in a heavy-bottomed saucepan over a medium flame. When hot, put in the onion. Stir and fry until the onion bits have browned lightly. Add the rice, green chilli, garlic, *garam masala* and salt. Stir gently for 3–4 minutes until all the grains are coated with oil. If the rice begins to stick to the bottom of the pan, turn the heat down slightly. Now pour in the stock and bring the rice to a boil. Cover with a very tight-fitting lid, turn heat to very, very low and cook for 25 minutes.

If you prefer, you could put the pan in a preheated gas mark 3, 325°F (170°C) oven for 25 minutes.

Simple buttery rice with onion

Pyaz wali basmati chaaval

This simple method of cooking rice makes it extremely versatile. You could serve it with Indian and English meals.

Serves 6:

2 oz (50g) unsalted butter

3 oz (75g) onion, peeled and chopped

Long-grain rice measured to the 15 fl oz (425ml) level in a glass measuring jug

1 teaspoon salt

$1\frac{1}{4}$ pints (700ml) water

Melt the butter in a heavy pot over a medium flame. When hot, put in the onion. Stir and sauté it until it is almost translucent. Do not let it brown in the slightest. Put in the rice and the salt. Stir and sauté gently for a minute. Pour in the water and bring to a boil. Cover tightly, turn heat to very, very low and let the rice cook for 25 minutes.

Rice with peas

Tahiri

This rice dish is flavoured, very mildly, with cumin seeds, making it suitable for almost any kind of meal.

Serves 6:

Long-grain rice measured to the 15 fl oz (425ml) level in a glass measuring jug

3 tablespoons vegetable oil

1 teaspoon whole cumin seeds

3 oz (75g) onion, peeled and finely chopped

5–6 oz (150–175g) fresh, shelled peas (frozen, defrosted peas may be substituted)

1 teaspoon salt

1 pint (570ml) water

Wash the rice in several changes of water and drain. Put the rice in a bowl. Add 2 pints (1.125 litres) water and soak for half an hour. Drain.

Heat the oil in a heavy pot over a medium flame. When hot, put in the cumin seeds. Stir them about for 3 seconds. Now put in the chopped onions. Stir and fry them until they get flecked with brown spots. Add the peas, rice, and salt. Stir and sauté gently for 3–4 minutes or until the peas and rice are coated with oil. Add 1 pint (570ml) water and bring to a boil. Cover very tightly, turn heat to very, very low and cook for 25 minutes. Turn off the flame and let the pot sit, covered and undisturbed, for another 5 minutes. Stir gently before serving.

Rice with yellow split peas
Khili hui khichri

Khichri is of ancient origin. I have read descriptions of it written by travellers who came to India as long as a thousand years ago. *Khichri* probably predates even these early travellers. It consists, basically, of rice and pulses cooked together and is served in most Indian homes in one of two forms, the 'wet', porridge-like version and the 'dry', grainy version. The recipe here is for the 'dry' *khichri* which my mother always referred to as *khili hui khichri* or 'the *khichri* which has bloomed'. This has the consistency of well-prepared rice. You could serve it with 'Lamb stew' (page 47) and an onion relish.

Serves 6:

2 oz (50g) yellow split peas, picked over, washed, and drained

Long-grain rice measured to the 15 fl oz (425ml) level in a glass measuring jug

3 tablespoons ghee (see page 25) or vegetable oil

½ teaspoon whole cumin seeds

½ teaspoon garam masala (see page 18)

1 teaspoon salt – or to taste

4 tablespoons finely chopped fresh coriander (fresh parsley may be substituted)

1 pint (570ml) chicken stock (water may be substituted)

Soak the split peas in ¾ pint (425ml) water for 3 hours. Drain. Wash the rice in several changes of water and drain. Soak in 2 pints (1.25 litres) water for 1 hour. Drain.

Heat the *ghee* in a heavy pot over a medium flame. When hot, put in the cumin seeds. Stir them around for a few seconds. Now put in the drained split peas and rice. Stir and sauté for 2–3 minutes or until the grains are coated with the *ghee*. Add the *garam masala*, salt, and fresh coriander. Stir and sauté for another minute or so. Add the chicken stock and bring to a boil. Cover tightly, turn heat to very, very low and cook for 25 minutes. Turn off the heat and let the pot sit, covered and undisturbed, for another 10 minutes.

Stir gently with a slotted spoon or fork before serving.

Vegetable pullao

Sabzi pullao

Sometimes, when I want an all-vegetarian meal, I serve this pullao with 'Black-eyed beans with mushrooms' (page 128) and a yoghurt dish. It can, of course, be served with any meat.

Serves 6:

Long-grain rice measured to the 15 fl oz (425ml) level in a glass measuring jug
4 oz (110g) potato, peeled
$\frac{1}{2}$ medium-sized carrot, about $1\frac{1}{2}$ oz (40g) in all, peeled
$1\frac{1}{2}$ oz (40g) fresh green beans
4 tablespoons vegetable oil
1 teaspoon whole cumin seeds
$1\frac{1}{4}$ teaspoon salt
$\frac{1}{2}$ teaspoon ground turmeric
1 teaspoon ground cumin seeds
1 teaspoon ground coriander seeds
$\frac{1}{4}$ teaspoon cayenne pepper
$\frac{1}{2}$ fresh hot green chilli, finely chopped
2 tablespoons very finely chopped fresh coriander
$\frac{1}{2}$ teaspoon peeled and very finely grated fresh ginger
1 clove garlic, peeled and mashed to a pulp
1 pint (570ml) water

Put the rice in a bowl and wash in several changes of water. Drain. Add 2 pints (1.25 litres) water and leave to soak for 30 minutes. Drain and leave in a sieve for 20 minutes.

Cut the potato and carrot into $\frac{1}{4}$ inch (5mm) dice. Trim the green beans and cut, crosswise, at $\frac{1}{4}$ inch (5mm) intervals.

Heat the oil in a heavy pot over a medium heat. When hot, put in the cumin seeds. Let them sizzle for 5–6 seconds. Now put in the potato, carrot, and green beans. Stir and sauté for a minute. Turn the heat to medium-low and add the drained rice, salt, turmeric, ground cumin, ground coriander, cayenne, green chilli, fresh coriander, ginger, and garlic. Stir and sauté the rice for 2–3 minutes. Add 1 pint (570ml) water and bring to a boil. Cover very tightly, turn heat to very, very low, and cook for 25 minutes. Turn off the heat and let the pot sit, covered and undisturbed, for another 10 minutes.

Mushroom pullao

Khumbi pullao

My mother used to make this dish with morel mushrooms. If you have some growing in your local woods, do, by all means, use them. Just slice them in half, lengthwise. You could also use the darker field mushrooms. In that case you would need to slice the caps. I tend to make this dish very frequently and find myself using the more easily available cultivated mushrooms. It is still a superb dish and may be served with almost any meat dish in this book. You could also serve it with a roast leg of lamb or with lamb chops.

Serves 6:

Long-grain rice measured to the 15 fl oz (425ml) level in a glass measuring jug

5 oz (150g) mushrooms

2 oz (50g) onion, peeled

3 tablespoons vegetable oil

1 clove garlic, peeled and finely chopped

½ teaspoon peeled and finely grated fresh ginger

¼ teaspoon garam masala (see page 18)

1 teaspoon salt

1 pint (570ml) water

Wash the rice in several changes of water and drain. Put the rice in a bowl. Add 2 pints (1.25 litres) water and soak for half an hour. Drain.

Wipe the mushrooms with a dampened cloth or kitchen paper. Cut the mushrooms, from the caps down to the stems, into ⅛ inch (3mm) thick slices. Cut the onion into half, lengthwise, and then crosswise into very thin slices.

Heat the oil in a heavy pot over a medium flame. When hot, put in the onions and garlic. Stir and fry for about 2 minutes or until the onions begin to turn brown at the edges. Put in the mushrooms and stir for another 2 minutes. Now put in the rice, ginger, *garam masala*, and salt. Turn heat to medium-low. Stir and sauté the rice for 2 minutes. Pour in 1 pint (570ml) water and bring to a boil. Cover very tightly, turn heat to very, very low and cook for 25 minutes. Turn off the heat and let the pot sit, covered and undisturbed, for another 5 minutes.

Aromatic yellow rice

Peelay chaaval

You may use either basmati rice or American long-grain rice for this recipe. The yellow colour, here, comes from ground turmeric. I like to serve it with 'Chicken in a red pepper sauce' (page 79) and 'Gujerati-style green beans' (page 102) just to get a wonderful contrast of bright colours.

Serves 6:

Long-grain or basmati rice measured to the 15 fl oz (425ml) level in a glass measuring jug

1 pint (570ml) water

1¼ teaspoons salt

¾ teaspoon ground turmeric

3–4 whole cloves

A 1 inch (2.5cm) stick of cinnamon

3 bay leaves

3 tablespoons unsalted butter, cut into small pats

Put the rice in a bowl and wash in several changes of water. Drain. Pour 2 pints (1.125 litres) fresh water over the rice and let it soak for half an hour. Drain the rice in a sieve.

Combine the drained rice, 1 pint (570ml) water, salt, turmeric, cloves, cinnamon, and bay leaves in a heavy pot and bring to a boil. Cover with a tight-fitting lid, turn heat to very, very low, and cook for 25 minutes. Let the pot rest, covered and undisturbed for 10 minutes. Add the small pats of butter to the rice and mix them in gently with a fork. Remove the whole spices before serving.

Lamb and rice casserole

Mughlai lamb biryani

Biryanis are grand, festive casseroles in which partially cooked rice is layered over cooked meat. Orange saffron milk is dribbled over the top, thereby colouring some grains yellow while leaving others white, and the dish set to bake in a slow oven. As it cooks, the *biryani* gets quite perfumed with saffron.

These days, with saffron being as expensive as it is, many people, even in India, use yellow food colouring as a substitute. You may also do so if you wish. Just use 1 teaspoon yellow liquid food colouring diluted with 1 teaspoon water instead of the saffron and warm milk.

Soaking the rice in salted water for long periods, from 3 to 24 hours, is an ancient trick that Persians have used to get rice grains as white – and as separate from each other – as possible. These shining white grains then contrast even better with those tinted with saffron.

A *biryani* is really a meal in itself and may be eaten with just a yoghurt dish, such as 'Yoghurt with aubergines' (page 164), and a relish, such as my 'Tomato, onion, and green coriander relish' (page 172). However, since *biryanis* are generally served at feasts and banquets, we tend to be somewhat lavish. At such occasions, it would not be at all amiss to serve the condiments suggested above *as well as* 'Chicken in a red pepper sauce' (page 79) and 'Cauliflower with onion and tomato' (page 108).

C.I.A (Culinary Institute of America)

1) measure to 15 fluid oz mark (in jug) - long grain rice.

In muslin bag
- 1 cinnamon stick
- slices fresh ginger
- cardamom pods - crush
- 1t Saffron

In large pot
3.5 litres of water.

simmer bag x 30 M / add rice & cook ½ done, drain, reserve 1 c

Saute in a little
- ~~chicken thighs~~ 2 cloves garlic
- 2 med. onions - cut ½ moons
= golden + crisp. (Remove)

add chicken Thigh = golden (only ½ cook)

Grind
- ½t Bl. pepper corns
- 1t cumin seeds
- ⅛t N/meg
- 1 T curry powder

whizz — V. fine sprinkle over chicken

Puree
- 2 x onions
- 4 cloves garlic
- ½" fresh ginger
- ¼ c water

Smooth, add Sultanas mix

To set up

In large pan - melt 2 nuts Butter, layer ⅓ of rice, chicken thighs (remove skin), ½ minced onions, ⅓ rice, Puree, ⅓ rice. Top ½ Yogurt / Butter

on med. heat,
cook until done. add
reserved rice water.
Put on lid

To serve
cilantro chopped
mint   "
S + P.

Serves 6:

Long-grain rice measured to the 15 fl oz (425ml) level in a glass measuring jug

About 3 tablespoons salt

1 teaspoon saffron threads

2 tablespoons warm milk

3 medium-sized onions, peeled

4 cloves garlic, peeled

A $\frac{3}{4}$ inch (2cm) cube of fresh ginger, peeled and coarsely chopped

4 tablespoons blanched, slivered almonds

3 tablespoons plus $6\frac{1}{4}$ pints (3.6 litres) water

13 tablespoons vegetable oil

3 tablespoons sultanas

$1\frac{1}{2}$ lb (700g) boned lamb meat from the shoulder, cut into 1 inch (2.5cm) cubes

8 fl oz (225ml) plain yoghurt

5–6 whole cloves

$\frac{1}{2}$ teaspoon whole black peppercorns

$\frac{1}{2}$ teaspoon whole cardamom seeds

1 teaspoon whole cumin seeds

1 teaspoon whole coriander seeds

A 1 inch (2.5cm) stick of cinnamon

About $\frac{1}{6}$ of a nutmeg

$\frac{1}{4}$ teaspoon cayenne pepper

1 oz (25g) unsalted butter, cut into 8 pieces

3 hard boiled eggs, peeled and at room temperature

Wash the rice in several changes of water. Drain it and put it in a large bowl. Add $3\frac{1}{2}$ pints (2 litres) water and 1 tablespoon salt. Mix and soak for 3 hours.

Put the saffron threads in a small, heavy (preferably cast iron) frying pan set over a medium flame. Toss the threads about until they turn a few shades darker. Put the warm milk in a small cup. Crumble the saffron into the warm milk and let it soak for 3 hours.

Cut two of the onions in half, lengthwise, and then cut the halves into fine half-rings. Set these aside. Chop the remaining onion very coarsely. Put this chopped onion, garlic, ginger, 2 tablespoons of the almonds, and 3 tablespoons water into the container of an electric blender. Blend until you have a paste.

Heat 6 tablespoons of the oil in a 10-inch (25cm), preferably non-stick frying pan over a medium-high flame. When hot, put in the onion half-rings. Stir and fry them until they are brown and crisp. Remove them with a slotted spoon and spread them out on a plate lined with kitchen paper.

Put the sultanas into the same oil. Remove them as soon as they turn plump – which happens immediately. Put the sultanas in another plate lined with absorbant paper. Put the remaining 2 tablespoons almonds into the oil. Stir and fry them until they are golden. Remove them with a slotted spoon and spread them out beside the sultanas. Set aside for use as the garnish.

Now put the meat cubes, a few at a time, into the same hot oil and brown them on all sides. As each batch gets done, put it in a bowl.

Add another 7 tablespoons oil to the frying pan and turn heat to medium. When hot, put in the onion-garlic-ginger-almond paste from the blender. Fry, stirring all the time, until the paste turns a medium brown colour. If it sticks slightly to the bottom of the pan, sprinkle in a little water and keep stirring. Return the meat and any accumulated juices to the pan. Add the yoghurt, a tablespoon at a time, stirring well between each addition. Now put in $1\frac{1}{4}$ teaspoon salt and $\frac{1}{4}$ pint (150ml) water. Mix and bring to a simmer. Cover, turn heat to low and simmer for 30 minutes.

While the meat is cooking, put the cloves, peppercorns, cardamom seeds, cumin seeds, coriander seeds, cinnamon, and nutmeg into the container of a spice grinder or a clean coffee grinder. Grind finely.

When the meat has cooked for 30 minutes, add all the spices from the spice grinder as well as the cayenne and mix well. Cover again and continue to cook on low heat for another 30 minutes. Remove cover, raise heat to medium, and cook, stirring all the time, until you have about 7 fl oz (200ml) of thick sauce left at the bottom of the pan. Turn off the heat and spoon off as much grease as possible. The meat should be pretty well cooked by now.

Spread out the meat and sauce in the bottom of a heavy casserole. Cover and keep warm.

Preheat oven to gas mark 2, 300°F (150°C).

Bring 6 pints (3.5 litres) of water to a rolling boil in a large pot. Add $1\frac{1}{2}$ tablespoons salt to it. Drain the rice and rinse it off under running water. Slowly, scatter the rice into the boiling water. Bring to a boil again and boil rapidly for exactly 6 minutes. Then drain the rice.

Work fast now. Put the rice on top of the meat, piling it up in the shape of a hill. Take a chopstick or the handle of a long spoon and make a 1 inch (2.5cm) wide hole going down like a well from the peak of the rice hill to its bottom. Dribble the saffron milk in streaks along the sides of the hill. Lay the pieces of butter on the sides of the hill and scatter 2 tablespoons of the browned onions over it as well. Cover first with aluminium foil, sealing the edges well, and then with a lid. Bake in the oven for 1 hour.

Remove from the oven. If left in a warm place, this rice will stay hot for 30 minutes.

Just before you get ready to serve, quarter the eggs, lengthwise. Mix the contents of the rice pot gently. Serve the rice on a warmed platter, garnished with the eggs, remaining browned onions, sultanas and almonds.

Sweet yellow rice
Meetha pullao

This wonderful, shining rice may be eaten by itself, with hot, spicy Indian dishes or even with English foods such as baked ham and roast goose.

Saffron does give this dish a very special flavour but if you are on a tight budget and find saffron a bit too expensive, just leave it (and the milk) out and increase the yellow food colouring to 1 teaspoon.

Serves 4:
½ teaspoon saffron threads
2 tablespoons warm milk
Basmati rice measured to the 8 fl oz (225ml) level in a glass measuring jug
2 oz (50g) ghee (see page 25) or unsalted butter
4 whole cardamom pods
A 1 inch (2.5cm) stick of cinnamon
¼ teaspoon liquid yellow food colouring
½ pint (275ml) water
½ teaspoon salt
3½ oz (90g) sugar, depending upon taste
½ oz (15g) blanched, slivered almonds
1 tablespoon sultanas

Put the saffron in a small heavy frying pan set over a medium flame. Stir it about until the threads turn a few shades darker. Put the milk in a small cup and crumble the saffron into it. Set it aside for 3 hours.

Wash the rice in several changes of water and drain it. Leave it to soak in 2 pints (1.25 litres) of water for half an hour. Drain for 20 minutes.

Preheat oven to gas mark 2, 300°F (150°C).

Heat the *ghee* in a wide, heavy, flame and oven-proof pot over a medium flame. When hot, put in the cardamom and cinnamon. Stir them about for a second. Now put in the rice. Stir and sauté the rice gently for about 3 minutes, turning the heat down slightly if it begins to catch. Add ½ pint (275ml) water, the yellow colouring and the salt. Turn the heat back to medium. Gently stir and cook the rice until all the water is absorbed. Put in the saffron milk, almonds, sultanas, and sugar. Stir to mix, cover very tightly, and put the pot in the oven for 30 minutes. Remove from oven and stir to mix.

Remove the cardamom and cinnamon before serving. If liked, silver vark (see page 22) can be placed on the rice with a few sultanas and nuts on top.

RELISHES, CHUTNEYS AND PICKLES

We like to perk up our meals in India with a variety of condiments. Their function, apart from teasing the palate with their sharp contrasts of sweet, sour, hot, and salty flavours, is to balance out the meal with added protein and vitamins.

Sometimes, these condiments can be quite simple – cucumber wedges seasoned quickly with salt, pepper, cayenne, and lemon juice or chopped up onions and tomatoes. At other times we can serve pickles that have taken weeks or months to mature. Some condiments, such as the 'Fresh coriander chutney' or the 'Gujerati carrot salad', should be eaten up within 48 hours. Others, such as the 'Apple, peach and apricot chutney' and the 'Cauliflower and white radish pickle', may be kept for a year.

Yoghurt relishes fall into another category. They can be condiments or they can be substantial dishes by themselves. Almost any herb or vegetable can be put into yoghurt, from mint to potatoes. Whenever I am serving an all Indian meal, I nearly always serve a yoghurt relish because it provides a cooling contrast.

Plain yoghurt

Dahi

Yoghurt is used in India for marinading meats – it tenderizes them, as a tart, creamy flavouring, and as an ingredient for sauces. As it is rich in protein, it is also eaten at almost every meal, either plain or mixed with seasonings and vegetables. It is a food that is easy to digest, far easier than milk. It is also considered a food that 'settles' the stomach, especially when combined with plain rice.

Naturally, few respectable Indian homes are ever without it. Most of the time it is made at home, although it can be bought from the bazaar as well.

To make yoghurt at home, you need milk, either whole or fat free, and some 'starter'. This 'starter' is a few tablespoons of borrowed, leftover, or bought yoghurt. You also need a warm temperature that hovers between $85°$ and $100°$F $(30–38°$C). This is the temperature at which yoghurt sets best. As this is not England's temperature normally, it has to be approximated. You could put the yoghurt in a warm cupboard near the water heater or in the oven of a cooker with a pilot light. The yoghurt bowl is also quite amenable to being wrapped in a blanket. I frequently resort to the blanket method.

$1\frac{3}{4}$ pints (1 litre) milk
2 tablespoons plain yoghurt

Bring the milk to a boil in a heavy pot. As soon as the milk begins to rise, remove the pot from the cooker. Let the milk cool to anywhere between $100°$ and $110°$F $(38–43°$C). It should feel warm to the touch. If a film forms over the top, just stir it in.

Put the yoghurt in a 2 pint (1.25 litres) stainless steel or non-metallic bowl and beat it with a whisk until it is smooth and creamy. Slowly, add the warm milk, a little bit at a time and stirring as you do so. Cover the bowl and then wrap it in an old blanket or shawl without tilting it. Set it aside in a warm place free of draughts for 6–8 hours, or until yoghurt has set.

Store the yoghurt in a refrigerator. It should stay fresh for 4–5 days.

Yoghurt with cucumber and mint

Kheere ka raita

Here is a cooling yoghurt dish that can be served with all Indian meals. It also makes an excellent snack which can be stored in the refrigerator and then taken out whenever someone comes in complaining of being tired, hot, and hungry.

Serves 6:

20 fl oz (570ml) plain yoghurt

5 inches (13cm) of cucumber, peeled and coarsely grated

2 tablespoons of finely chopped fresh mint

$\frac{1}{2}$ teaspoon ground, roasted cumin seeds (see page 17)

$\frac{1}{4}$ teaspoon cayenne pepper

1 teaspoon salt

Freshly ground black pepper

Put the yoghurt in a bowl. Beat lightly with a fork or whisk until smooth and creamy. Add all the other ingredients and mix. Cover and refrigerate until ready to eat.

Yoghurt with walnuts and fresh coriander

Akhrote ka raita

Another cooling, nourishing dish. It may be eaten by itself or served with Indian meals.

Serves 6:

20 fl oz (570ml) plain yoghurt

2 tablespoons finely chopped fresh coriander

½ fresh hot green chilli, very finely chopped

About ½ teaspoon salt – or to taste

Freshly ground black pepper

1 spring onion, very finely sliced

2½ oz (60g) shelled walnuts, broken up, roughly, into ⅓–½ inch (1–2cm) pieces

Put the yoghurt in a bowl. Beat lightly with a fork or a whisk until it is smooth and creamy. Add all the other ingredients. Stir to mix.

Yoghurt with aubergines

Baigan ka raita

Here is a soothing, cooling, and exceedingly simple way to serve aubergines. I like to serve this with 'Lamb cooked with potatoes' (page 54), 'Gujerati-style green beans' (page 102) and either rice or an Indian bread.

Serves 6:

1 medium-sized – 1¼ lb (560g) aubergine, peeled and cut into 1 inch (2.5cm) cubes

20 fl oz (570ml) plain yoghurt

¾ teaspoon salt, or to taste

Freshly ground black pepper

⅛ teaspoon cayenne pepper, optional

1 spring onion, washed and cut into paper-thin rounds all the way up its green section

1 tablespoon finely chopped fresh mint

A few mint leaves for garnishing

Bring water in the bottom part of a steaming utensil to the boil. (If you do not have a steaming utensil, set a steaming trivet or a colander inside a large pot. Pour water into the pot in such a way that it stays just below the lowest part of the trivet or colander. Bring this water to a boil.)

Put the aubergine cubes into the steamer section of your steaming utensil (or into the trivet or colander), cover and steam over high heat for 10 minutes. Make sure that your boiling water does not run out.

While the aubergine is steaming, put the yoghurt into a bowl and beat it lightly with a fork or a whisk until it is smooth and creamy. Add the salt, pepper, cayenne, spring onion, and mint to it. Mix with a fork.

Lift out the steamed aubergine pieces and mash with a fork. Spread out the aubergine in a plate and leave to cool somewhat (or else the yoghurt would curdle).

Fold the aubergine into the yoghurt and garnish with mint leaves.

Gujerati-style yoghurt with potatoes

Batata nu raita

This is an Indian potato salad except that we use seasoned yoghurt as a dressing instead of mayonnaise or a vinaigrette. In order to make the yoghurt very thick and creamy, it is generally hung up in a cheesecloth for an hour. You may omit this step if you are in a rush. You will, of course, end up with a more 'flowing' sauce, rather than one which clings to the potatoes.

It may be served with 'Minced meat with peas' (page 44) and an Indian bread.

Serves 4:

10 oz (275g) potatoes

15 fl oz (425ml) plain yoghurt

$\frac{1}{2}$ teaspoon salt

Freshly ground black pepper

2 tablespoons vegetable oil

1 teaspoon whole cumin seeds

$\frac{1}{8}$ teaspoon cayenne pepper – or to taste

Optional garnish: 1 tablespoon finely chopped fresh coriander

Boil the potatoes in their jackets. Drain them and let them cool for at least an hour.

Set a sieve over a bowl and line it with a 15–16 inch (38–40cm) square of doubled cheesecloth, muslin or a clean tea towel. Put the yoghurt into the cheesecloth. Now bring the four corners of the cheesecloth together. Use one of the corners to tie the cheesecloth into a bundle. Hang this bundle somewhere so it can drip for an hour. I usually hang it from the tap in my sink. Do not squeeze the cheesecloth. Just let it drip on its own.

Empty the yoghurt into a bowl. Add about $\frac{1}{4}$ teaspoon salt and some black pepper. Beat lightly with a fork or a whisk until the yoghurt is smooth and creamy. Taste for seasonings.

Peel the potatoes and cut them into $\frac{3}{4}$ inch (2cm) dice. Heat the oil in a frying pan (non-stick is best) over a medium flame. When hot, put in the cumin seeds. Let the cumin seeds sizzle for 3–4 seconds. Now put in the diced potatoes, about $\frac{1}{3}$ teaspoon salt, some black pepper and the cayenne. Stir and cook the potatoes for about 4 minutes. Taste a potato piece for salt and other seasonings. You may make this dish as hot as you like. Take the frying pan off the heat and let the potatoes cool for 5 minutes. Pour the contents of the frying pan – oil, spices and potatoes – into the bowl with the yoghurt. Stir to mix and garnish, if you like, with fresh coriander or parsley.

Fresh coriander chutney

Hare dhaniye ki chutney

This is the kind of chutney that is made fresh in our homes every day. Apart from its sharp, perky taste, it is exceedingly rich in Vitamins A and C as well as in chlorophyll. We eat small amounts – 1–2 teaspoons – with our meals, just as you might eat mustard with sausages. It also serves as an excellent dip for snacks such as *samosas*.

When making the chutney, use just the top, leafy sections of the coriander plant. The lower stems get too stringy when pulverized.

Serves 4–6:

3 oz (75g) fresh green coriander (weight without lower stems and roots), coarsely chopped

½–1 fresh, hot green chilli, coarsely chopped

1½ tablespoons lemon juice

½ teaspoon salt

½ teaspoon ground roasted cumin seeds (see page 17)

Freshly ground black pepper

Combine all ingredients in the container of an electric blender. Blend, pushing down with a rubber spatula several times, until you have a paste. Empty the paste into a small glass or other non-metallic bowl.

OPPOSITE PAGE:
Cocktail koftas, *Chhote kofte* (page 184)
Fried cashews, *Tale huay caju* (page 181)
Spicy matchstick potatoes, *Aloo ka tala hua laccha* (page 190)
Quick fried prawns, *Tali hui jhinga* (page 187)

Apple, peach and apricot chutney

Sev, aroo, aur kubani ki chutney

This superb fruity sweet-and-sour chutney has the thick consistency of a preserve and may be bottled and kept for long periods. Those who like their chutney very hot can add up to $1\frac{1}{2}$ teaspoons of cayenne pepper. It may be served with all Indian meals as well as with gammon roasts, pork chops, and ham.

Makes about $1\frac{1}{4}$ pints (750ml):

$1\frac{1}{4}$ lb (500g) sour cooking apples, peeled, cored and coarsely chopped

4 oz (110g) dried peaches, quartered

4 oz (110g) dried apricots

2 oz (50g) sultanas

6 cloves garlic, peeled and mashed to a pulp

Two 1-inch (2.5cm) cubes of fresh ginger, peeled and finely grated

14 fl oz (400ml) white wine vinegar

14 oz (385g) castor sugar

2 teaspoons salt

$\frac{1}{2}$ teaspoon cayenne pepper

Combine all the ingredients in a heavy stainless steel or porcelain-lined pot and bring to a boil. Turn heat to medium-low and cook, keeping up a fairly vigorous simmer, for about 30 minutes or until you have a thick, jamlike consistency. Stir frequently and turn the heat down slightly when the chutney thickens as it could stick to the bottom of the pot.

Let the chutney cool. It will thicken some more as it cools. Pour into a clean jar and cover with a non-metallic lid. Store in a cool place or keep in the refrigerator.

OPPOSITE PAGE:
Fresh mango slices (page 195)
Carrot halva, *Gajar ka halva* (page 193)
Spiced tea, *Masala chai* (page 196)
Ice cream with nuts, *Kulfi* (page 193)

Gujerati carrot salad

Gajar ka salad

This simple, lightly spiced, easy-to-make salad may be served with Indian meals – or with something as British as grilled sausages! There are many variations to it which you might like to try out on your family and friends. You could, for example, leave out the lemon juice. This highlights the natural sweetness of the carrots. Or you could add 2 tablespoons of sultanas which you should soak in hot water for 2–3 hours first.

Serves 4:

¾ lb (350g) carrots, trimmed, peeled and grated coarsely

¼ teaspoon salt

2 tablespoons vegetable oil

1 tablespoon whole black mustard seeds

2 teaspoons lemon juice

In a bowl, toss the grated carrots with the salt. Heat the oil in a very small pan over a medium flame. When very hot, put in the mustard seeds. As soon as the mustard seeds begin to pop (this takes just a few seconds), pour the contents of the pan – oil and seeds, over the carrots. Add the lemon juice and toss.

You may serve this salad at room temperature or cold.

Carrot and onion salad

Gajar aur pyaz ka salad

This salad is made with the deep red, beetroot-like 'bleeding' carrot that is found in north India during the winter months. I have substituted the ordinary orange carrot. It may be served with nearly all Indian meals.

Serves 6:

3 carrots, weighing about $\frac{1}{2}$ lb (225g) in all
3 oz (75g) onion, peeled
$\frac{3}{4}$ teaspoon salt
Freshly ground black pepper
4 teaspoons lemon juice
$\frac{1}{8}$–$\frac{1}{4}$ teaspoon cayenne pepper
$\frac{1}{2}$ teaspoon peeled and finely grated fresh ginger

Peel the carrots and cut them, crosswise and at a diagonal, into $\frac{1}{8}$ inch (3mm) thick oval slices. Cut the slices, lengthwise, into $\frac{1}{8}$ inch (3mm) wide strips.

Halve the onion, lengthwise, and then cut it crosswise into $\frac{1}{8}$ inch (3mm) thick slices.

Bring 4 pints (2.25 litres) of water to a rolling boil. Throw in the carrots. Bring to a boil again. Boil rapidly for 2 seconds only. Drain the carrots immediately and rinse them under cold, running water. Drain again.

Combine the carrots, onions, salt, black pepper, lemon juice, cayenne pepper, and ginger. Stir to mix.

This salad may be served as soon as it is made or several hours later. It may be served at room temperature or cold.

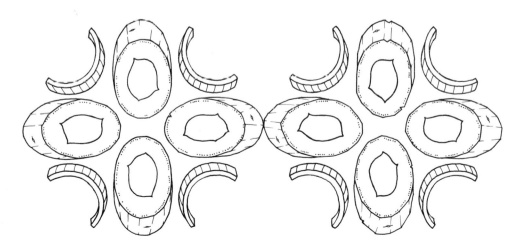

Spicy cucumber wedges

Kheere ke tukray

These wedges are refreshing and deliciously crunchy and may be served with any Indian meal. It is best to prepare them at the last minute, just before you sit down to eat.

Serves 4:

10 oz (275g) cucumber – about 10 inches (25cm) of cucumber

$\frac{1}{3}$ teaspoon salt

$\frac{1}{8}$ teaspoon cayenne pepper

Freshly ground black pepper

$\frac{1}{3}$ teaspoon ground, roasted cumin seeds (see page 17)

The juice of about $\frac{3}{4}$ of a lemon

Peel the cucumber and cut it into half, crosswise. Now cut each half into 4 sections, lengthwise. Arrange the wedges on a plate. Sprinkle the salt, cayenne, black pepper, cumin, and lemon juice over them. Serve immediately.

Tomato, onion and green coriander relish

Cachumber

This tasy relish complements almost all Indian meals.

Serves 4–6:

$\frac{1}{2}$ lb (225g) tomatoes

3 oz (75g) onion, peeled

4 heaped tablespoons chopped fresh coriander (fresh parsley may be substituted)

$\frac{3}{4}$ teaspoon salt

2 tablespoons lemon juice

$\frac{1}{2}$ teaspoon cayenne pepper

$\frac{1}{2}$ teaspoon ground roasted cumin seeds (see page 17)

Cut the tomatoes and onions into $\frac{1}{4}$ inch (5mm) dice and put them in a smallish, non-metallic serving bowl. Add all the other ingredients and mix.

Cauliflower and white radish pickle

Phool gobi aur mooli ka achaar

This is one of the simplest Indian pickles. It does take several days to mature, so you have to be patient. Small amounts of it may be served at all Indian meals.

You may substitute turnip slices for the white radish in this recipe. The mustard seeds and oil, however, are essential. I heat the mustard oil before I use it in the pickle, because this process transforms it from a pungent oil to a sweet one.

Will fill a $1\frac{1}{2}$ pint (850ml) jar:

$\frac{1}{2}$ lb (225g) cauliflower

$\frac{1}{2}$ lb (225g) white radish (weight without leaves)

4 teaspoons whole black mustard seeds

4 fl oz (110ml) mustard or vegetable oil

2 teaspoons salt

$\frac{1}{2}$ teaspoon ground turmeric

$\frac{1}{2}$–1 teaspoon cayenne pepper

Cut the cauliflower into slim flowerettes that are 1–$1\frac{1}{2}$ inches (3cm) across at the head, $\frac{1}{3}$–$\frac{1}{2}$ inch (1cm) wide and $1\frac{1}{2}$–2 inches (4–5cm) in length. Peel the radish and cut it into $\frac{1}{3}$ inch (1cm) thick rounds. If the diameter of the slices is more than 1 inch (2.5cm), halve or quarter the slices.

Grind the mustard seeds coarsely in a coffee-grinder or other spice grinder.

Heat the oil in a small pot or frying pan over a medium heat. As soon as it gets very, very hot, turn off the heat and let it cool. (Remembering to take very great care with hot oil – stand over the oil as it cools.)

Put the cut vegetables in a bowl. Add the ground mustard seeds, salt, turmeric and cayenne. Mix well. Add the oil and mix again. Empty the contents of the bowl into a 2 pint (1.25 litres) glass or ceramic jar and cover with a non-metallic lid. For the next few days, put the jar in a warm, sunny spot in the day time and, if that spot is outdoors, bring the jar in at night. This pickle may take 4–5 days to mature in the summer and about 8 days in the winter.

Make sure you shake the jar at least 3–4 times a day. When the pickle is sour enough for your liking, it is ready. You may store it in a cool part of the kitchen.

Onion relish

Pyaz ka laccha

This is one of those relishes that may be served with almost every Indian meal. It may be familiar to you from Indian restaurants where it is sometimes described as 'onion chutney'.

Serves 4:

4 oz (110g) onion, peeled
¾ teaspoon salt
4 teaspoons lemon juice
¼ teaspoon paprika (the redder in colour, the better)
⅛ teaspoon cayenne pepper

Cut the onion, crosswise, into paper-thin rings. Put the rings into a bowl. Add all the other ingredients. Toss and mix. Set aside for 30 minutes (or more) before eating, in order to let the flavours blend.

Crisp, browned onions

Bhuni hui pyaz

These onions, when sprinkled over cooked foods, serve as a flavourful garnish. When crumbled and added to sauces for meats and vegetables, they provide a distinctive texture, taste, and colour.

Enough to fill a ½ pint (275ml) jar:

6 oz (175g) onions, peeled
Vegetable oil for shallow frying

Cut the onions into half, lengthwise. Now cut them, crosswise, into very, very thin, even slices.

Heat about ½ inch (1cm) of oil in an 8–9 inch (20–23cm) frying pan over a medium flame. When hot, put in all the onions. Stir and fry the onions until they turn reddish brown in colour. Remove them with a slotted spoon and spread them out on a plate lined with absorbent kitchen paper. As the onions cool, they should turn quite crisp. They may be eaten the same day or else stored in a tightly closed container for a few days.

SOUPS, SNACKS, SAVOURIES AND SWEETS

Indians love to munch. Whether they are on buses, trains, cinema houses or in parks, they can be spotted opening up newspaper cones, unwrapping tea-cloth bundles or easing eager hands into terra cotta pots. Good things are hidden inside that can be nibbled upon for the satisfaction of the soul.

Take *samosas*, for instance, those triangular, savoury pastries. The best place to eat them is right on the street, when the odours wafting from a near-by *samosa*-maker become too overwhelming to resist. All kinds of *kebabs*, marinated and grilled meat cubes, are also sold at open stalls. This is done deliberately to entice passing strollers.

All workers in India stop for tea, a custom not too different from the British one. But what is served, *is* a bit different. There would be tea of course, perhaps *masala chai* ('Spiced tea') or coffee. Then, an odd assortment might appear – *samosas*, fried cashews, and, to sweeten the mouth, some carrot halva!

All these dishes have been included in this chapter. There are also snacks that may be served with drinks, such as cocktail *koftas* (meatballs) that lend themselves very well to having toothpicks stuck in them and spicy potato matchsticks.

I have included some soups in this chapter as well. Even though we do not, as a nation drink soups, most Westernized Indians have happily adapted soups from other nations to suit their own tastes.

Everyday meals in India generally end with fresh fruit – mangoes, pineapples, oranges, apples, pears, bananas, guavas, cherries, loquats, melons, jackfruit – whatever happens to be in season. Fruit is refreshing and cleansing – and a perfect conclusion to a spicy meal.

In our family, my mother always peeled and cut the smaller fruit for all of us at the table. A plate was passed around and we took what we wanted. Larger, messier fruit, such as water melons, were cut in the kitchen before the meal and left to cool in the refrigerator.

Desserts and sweetmeats are usually reserved for festive occasions. A wedding banquet invariably brings forth large vats filled with *kulfi* – Indian ice cream – and at religious festivals some variety of halva is nearly always served.

Green soup

Hara shorva

This is India's version of cream of pea soup. It is delicate and quite delicious.

Makes 2½ pints (1.5 litres) and serves 5–6:

4 oz (110g) potato, peeled and roughly diced

3 oz (75g) onion, peeled and coarsely chopped

2 pints (1.25 litres) chicken stock

A ¾ inch (2cm) cube of fresh ginger, peeled

½ teaspoon ground coriander seeds

2 teaspoons ground cumin seeds

5 tablespoons chopped fresh coriander

½ fresh hot green chilli

10 oz (275g) shelled peas, fresh or frozen

¾ teaspoon salt (more if the stock is unsalted)

1 tablespoon lemon juice

½ teaspoon ground roasted cumin seeds (see page 17)

¼ pint (150ml) double cream

Combine the potato, onion, chicken stock, ginger, ground coriander, and ground cumin in a pot and bring to a boil. Cover, turn heat to low and simmer for 30 minutes. Fish out the cube of ginger and discard it. Add the fresh coriander, chilli, peas, salt, lemon juice, and roasted cumin. Bring to a boil and simmer, uncovered, for 2–3 minutes or until peas are just tender. Empty the soup into the container of an electric blender in two or three batches and blend until it is smooth. Put the soup into a clean pot. Add the cream and bring to a simmer to heat through.

Cold yoghurt soup with mint

Dahi ka shorva

Nothing could be more pleasant in the summer than this soothing, cooling soup that probably originated in the Caucasus and then came down to India with wandering Turks, Persians, and Moghuls.

Serves 4–6:

20 fl oz (570ml) plain yoghurt

$\frac{1}{2}$ pint (275ml) single cream

$\frac{3}{4}$ pint (425ml) cold, defatted chicken stock

$\frac{1}{2}$ teaspoon ground roasted cumin seeds (see page 17)

$\frac{1}{2}$ teaspoon salt (more if the stock is unsalted)

Freshly ground black pepper

2 teaspoons lemon juice

1 tablespoon very, very finely chopped fresh mint or 1 teaspoon dried mint flakes, crumbled into a powder

Put the yoghurt into a bowl. Beat lightly with a fork or a whisk until smooth and creamy. Pour in the cream. Beat gently to mix. Add the chicken stock, cumin, salt, black pepper, lemon juice, and mint. Stir to mix and taste for seasoning.

Chicken mulligatawny soup

There are many soupy dishes in India that are served with rice. It was probably one of these that inspired Anglo-Indian communities three centuries ago to create a soup that had Indian spices and ingredients in it, yet could be served at the start of a meal.

There are hundreds of recipes for mulligatawny soup in India, all slightly different. For this book, I have chosen one in which the base is a purée of red split lentils (*masoor dal*). It is a hearty soup that can almost be a meal in itself. I often have it for lunch with a simple green salad. It is traditional to have some plain boiled rice with this soup. I usually serve it on the side, in small quantities.

Serves 4–6:

6 oz (175g) red split lentils, picked over, washed, and drained

2 pints (1.25 litres) chicken stock

$\frac{1}{2}$ teaspoon ground turmeric

4 oz (110g) potato

1 chicken breast, boned and skinned, with a net weight of about 7 oz (200g)

$1\frac{1}{4}$ teaspoon salt

Freshly ground black pepper

5 cloves garlic, peeled

A $1\frac{1}{4}$ inch (3cm) cube of fresh ginger, peeled and coarsely chopped

$4\frac{1}{2}$ tablespoons plus 8 fl oz (225ml) water

3 tablespoons vegetable oil

1 teaspoon ground cumin seeds

1 teaspoon ground coriander seeds

$\frac{1}{8}$–$\frac{1}{4}$ teaspoon cayenne pepper

About 1 tablespoon lemon juice (you might want more)

Combine the lentils, chicken stock, and turmeric in a heavy, medium-sized pot and bring to a boil. Cover, leaving the lid just very slightly ajar, turn heat to low, and simmer gently for 30 minutes.

While the soup simmers, peel the potato and cut into $\frac{1}{2}$ inch (1cm) dice. When the soup has cooked for half an hour, add the cut potato to it. Cover, leaving the lid slightly ajar again, and continue the simmering for another 30 minutes.

During this second simmering period, put the garlic and ginger into the container of an electric blender. Add $4\frac{1}{2}$ tablespoons water and blend until you have a smooth paste.

Remove all fat from the chicken breast and cut it into $\frac{1}{2}$ inch (1cm) dice. Put the chicken in a bowl. Sprinkle $\frac{1}{4}$ teaspoon salt and some black pepper over it. Toss to mix.

Once the soup base has finished cooking, it needs to be puréed. I do this in a blender, in three batches. Put the puréed soup in a bowl. Add 1 teaspoon salt to it and mix.

Rinse and wipe out your soup pot. Pour the oil into it and set it over a medium flame. When the oil is hot, put in the garlic-ginger paste, the cumin, coriander, and cayenne. Fry, stirring continuously, until the spice mixture is slightly browned and separates from the oil. Put in the chicken pieces. Stir and fry another 2–3 minutes or until the chicken pieces turn quite opaque. Add 8 fl oz (225ml) water and bring to a boil. Cover, turn heat to low, and simmer for 3 minutes or until chicken is cooked. Pour in the puréed soup and the lemon juice. Stir to mix and bring to a simmer. Taste the soup for seasonings. I usually add another teaspoon or so of lemon juice. Simmer the soup very gently for another 2 minutes. If it is too thick, you can always thin it out with a little chicken stock or water.

Poppadum

Paapar

These thin, crisp discs are sold in markets either plain or flavoured with spices and seasonings such as garlic or black pepper or red pepper. They are partially prepared. A seasoned dough made from dried pulses has already been rolled out into the required shapes and then dried in the sun. All that you have to do is cook the poppadum. The cooking process is quick and easy.

There are two basic methods to choose from. Deep-frying is the traditional method. This allows the poppadums to expand to their fullest and turn very airy. It also brings out their full flavour. This method does, however, leave those who are nibbling the poppadum with slightly greasy fingers. The second method is to roast the poppadums directly over or under a flame. This way you end up with clean fingers and poppadums with fewer calories. But the poppadums do not expand as much and remain denser than fried ones.

Poppadums may be served with drinks or with Indian meals of any sort.

Serves 6:

The frying method:

6 poppadums

Vegetable oil for deep-frying

Depending upon the size of the poppadum, either leave them whole or snap each into two halves. Remember that they will expand in the frying pan.

Put about $\frac{3}{4}$ inch (2cm) of oil in a frying pan and set it to heat over a medium flame. When hot, put in a poppadum (or half a poppadum, depending upon the size of the frying pan and poppadum). It will sizzle and expand within seconds. Remove the poppadum with a slotted spoon and drain on kitchen paper. Cook all poppadum this way.

Poppadums should retain their yellowish colour and not turn brown. They should also cook very fast. Adjust your heat, if necessary.

The roasting method:

6 poppadum

Heat your grill. Put 1 poppadum on a rack and place it about 2–3 inches (5–7.5cm) under the grill. Now watch it very carefully. It will expand in seconds. It will also turn paler and develop a few bubbles. Turn it over and expose the second side to the flame for a second or so. Watch it all the time and do not let it brown or burn. Remove from the grill. Make all poppadum this way. (When making poppadum under a grill, it is not always necessary to turn it over. You will have to use your own judgement here.)

Poppadum may also be roasted directly on top of a live flame. Of course, you can only do this if you have a gas cooker. If you wish to follow this method, turn the flame on low. Now grip a poppadum with a set of tongs and hold it half an inch above the flame. The part of the poppadum that is directly over the flame will bubble and turn lighter in colour. When that happens, expose another part of the poppadum to the flame. Keep doing this until the entire poppadum has been roasted.

Fried cashews

Tale huay caju

Cashews that have been freshly fried at home have an exquisite taste, far better than that of the tinned and bottled variety. In India, this was the only kind of cashew we ate, with my mother frying the nuts just before my father sat down for his evening Scotch and soda.

Raw cashews can be bought at most health-food stores.

Serves 4–6:
Vegetable oil for deep-frying
$\frac{1}{2}$ lb (225g) raw cashew nuts
$\frac{1}{4}$ teaspoon salt
Freshly ground black pepper

Put a sieve on top of a metal bowl and set it near the stove. Also, line two plates with kitchen paper and set them nearby.

Heat about 1 inch (2.5cm) of oil in a deep, 8 inch (20cm) frying pan over a medium flame. When hot, put in all the cashews. Stir and fry them until they turn a reddish-gold colour. This happens fairly fast. Now empty the contents of the frying pan into the sieve to drain the oil. Lift up the sieve and shake out all the extra oil. Spread the cashews out on one of the plates and sprinkle the salt and pepper on them. Stir to mix. Now slide the cashews on to the second plate. This will take some more of the oil off them. Serve cashews warm or after they have cooled off.

Skewered chicken kebabs
Murghi tikka

You could serve these pieces of marinated and baked chicken as a first course or you could cut them in halves, stick toothpicks in them and pass them around with drinks. It has become traditional in Indian restaurants, where *Murghi tikka* is offered before the main course, to arrange the chicken pieces prettily on a platter and then surround them with thickly cut slices of onions sautéed very lightly in oil, some sliced cucumbers, and wedges of lime.

This dish belongs to the same family as Tandoori chicken and should, ideally, be cooked in a tandoor or clay oven. I find that ordinary home ovens, heated to their maximum temperature, make adequate substitutes.

Murghi tikka is a useful dish to have in one's repertoire. Most of the work – and it is not that much – can be done a day ahead of time. All that remains then is to brush the chicken pieces with butter and slip them into the oven for about 15 minutes.

Serves 4–6:

3 chicken breasts, boned and skinned – net weight after boning and skinning, about $2\frac{3}{4}$ lb (1kg 250g)

$1\frac{1}{4}$ teaspoons salt

One juicy lemon

6 tablespoons plain yoghurt

A 1 inch (2.5cm) cube of fresh ginger, peeled and finely grated

3 cloves garlic, peeled and mashed to a pulp

1 teaspoon ground cumin seeds

$\frac{1}{8}$–$\frac{1}{4}$ teaspoon cayenne pepper

$\frac{1}{4}$ teaspoon garam masala (see page 18)

2 teaspoons yellow liquid food colouring mixed with $\frac{1}{2}$ teaspoon red liquid food colouring

About 4 oz (110g) unsalted butter, melted

Remove all the fat from the chicken pieces. Cut each breast in half, lengthwise, and then cut each half, crosswise, into three or four, more or less equal pieces. Lay the pieces in a single layer on a platter. Sprinkle half the salt over them. Squeeze the juice from half the lemon over them as well. Rub the salt and lemon into the chicken. Turn the chicken pieces over and do the same on the second side with the remaining salt and lemon half. Set aside for 20 minutes.

Meanwhile, put the yoghurt in a small bowl. Beat it with a fork or whisk until it is smooth and creamy. Add the ginger, garlic, cumin, cayenne, and *garam masala*. Stir to mix.

After the chicken has sat around in its first marinade for 20 minutes, brush one side with the food colouring. Turn the chicken pieces over with a pair of tongs and brush the second side with the colouring. Put the chicken pieces and all accumulated juices in a bowl. Hold a sieve over the chicken pieces. Pour the yoghurt mixture into the sieve and then push through as much of it as you can with a rubber spatula. Fold this second marinade over the chicken pieces. Cover tightly and refrigerate for 6–24 hours.

Preheat your oven to its maximum temperature.

Thread the chicken pieces on skewers, leaving a little space between each piece. Balance the skewers on the raised rim of a baking tray, making sure that the meat juices will drip on to the tray and not your oven floor. Brush the chicken with half the melted butter and put in the oven for about 7 minutes. Take out the baking tray and skewers. Turn the chicken pieces over and brush again with butter. Bake another 8–10 minutes or until chicken is just done. Do not overcook.

Lamb or beef kebabs

Boti kabab

These kebabs make excellent nibbling fare for snacks.

Serves 4 as a snack:

8–9 oz (225–250g) boned lamb from shoulder or leg, or beef steak

4 tablespoons plain yoghurt

1½ tablespoons lemon juice

A 1 inch (2.5cm) cube of fresh ginger, peeled and very finely grated

1 clove garlic, peeled and mashed to a pulp

1 teaspoon ground cumin seeds

½ teaspoon ground coriander seeds

¼ teaspoon cayenne pepper

¾ teaspoon salt

1½ tablespoons vegetable oil

Cut the meat into ¾ inch (2cm) cubes and put in a stainless steel or other non-metallic bowl.

Combine the yoghurt, lemon juice, ginger, garlic, cumin, coriander, cayenne, and salt in a bowl and mix well with a fork. Hold a sieve over the meat and pour the yoghurt mixture into it. Push this mixture through the sieve, extracting all the paste that you can. Mix the meat and the marinade well. Cover and refrigerate for 6–24 hours.

Heat your grill.

Thread the meat on to skewers. Balance the skewers on the rim of a baking tray in such a way that all the meat juices drip inside the tray. Brush the kebabs generously with oil and place the baking tray under the grill. When one side of the meat gets lightly browned, turn the skewers to brown the opposite side, making sure to brush this side first with more oil.

Delicious cocktail koftas

Chhote kofte

Almost every country has some type of meatball. This Indian one is made out of minced lamb and you can eat it as part of a meal or you could stick toothpicks into the koftas and serve them as snacks.

Makes 30 meatballs and serves 6 for snacks, 4 for dinner:

For the meatballs:

1 lb (450g) minced lamb
½ teaspoon salt
1 teaspoon ground cumin seeds
1 teaspoon ground coriander seeds
¼ teaspoon garam masala (see page 18)
⅛ teaspoon cayenne pepper
2 tablespoons very finely chopped fresh coriander
3 tablespoons plain yoghurt

Combine all the ingredients for the meatballs. Dip your hands in water whenever you need to and form about 30 meatballs.

Put the garlic and ginger into the container of a food processor or blender along with 4 tablespoons water. Blend until you have a paste. Put the paste in a bowl. Add the cumin, ground coriander, paprika, and cayenne. Stir to mix.

For the sauce:

5 cloves garlic, peeled

A 1 inch (2.5cm) cube of fresh ginger, peeled and coarsely chopped

4 tablespoons plus ½ pint (275ml) water

½ teaspoon salt

1 teaspoon ground cumin seeds

1 teaspoon ground coriander seeds

1 teaspoon bright red paprika

¼ teaspoon cayenne pepper

5 tablespoons vegetable oil

A 1 inch (2.5cm) stick of cinnamon

6 whole cardamom pods

6 whole cloves

4 oz onion, peeled and finely chopped

4 oz (110g) tomato, peeled (see page 29) and chopped (a small tin of tomatoes may be substituted)

4 tablespoons plain yoghurt

Heat the oil in a heavy, 9–10 inch (23–25cm) wide pot or frying pan over a medium-high flame. When hot, put in the cinnamon, cardamom, and cloves. Stir them for 3–4 seconds. Now put in the onions, and fry them, stirring all the time, until they are reddish-brown in colour. Turn the heat to medium and put in the paste from the bowl as well as the chopped tomato. Stir and fry this mixture until it turns a brownish colour. When it begins to catch, add 1 tablespoon of yoghurt. Stir and fry some more until the yoghurt is incorporated into the sauce. Now add another tablespoon of yoghurt. Incorporate that into the sauce as well. Keep doing this until you have put in all the yoghurt. Now put in ½ pint (275ml) water and ½ teaspoon salt. Stir and bring to a simmer. Put in all the meatballs in a single layer. Cover, leaving the lid very slightly ajar, turn heat to low and cook for 25 minutes. Stir very gently every 5 minutes or so, making sure not to break the meatballs. Towards the end of the cooking period, you should scrape the bottom of the pot just to make sure the sauce is not catching. If necessary, add a tablespoon or so of water. Remove the lid and turn the heat up to medium low. Stir gently and cook until the meatballs have a browned look. All the sauce should now be clinging to the meatballs and there should be just a little fat left at the bottom of the pot.

When you are ready to eat, heat the koftas gently. Lift them out of the fat and shake off any whole spices that may be clinging to them. Stick a toothpick into each kofta if serving with drinks. If you have these koftas for dinner, you could leave more of a sauce.

Tandoori-style prawns

Tandoori jhinga

These marinated prawns are traditionally cooked in a tandoor. Since the prawns generally available in Britain tend to be small, I cook them very quickly in a frying pan. You may easily double the recipe, if you wish to serve these prawns as a main course. Just use a larger frying pan.

Serves 4 as a snack:

4 tablespoons plain yoghurt

A 1 inch (2.5cm) cube of fresh ginger, peeled and very finely grated

1 large clove garlic, peeled and mashed to a pulp

5 teaspoons lemon juice

¼ teaspoon salt – or to taste

Freshly ground black pepper

1½ teaspoons ground roasted cumin seeds (see page 17)

¼ teaspoon garam masala (see page 18)

2 teaspoons yellow liquid food colouring mixed with 1 teaspoon red liquid food colouring

8 oz (225g) peeled good quality prawns, defrosted and patted dry

2 oz (50g) unsalted butter

Put the yoghurt in a bowl. Beat lightly with a fork or a whisk until it is smooth and creamy. Add the ginger, garlic, lemon juice, salt, some black pepper, roasted cumin, *garam masala*, and liquid food colouring. Stir to mix and set aside for 15 minutes. Push this liquid through a sieve into a second bowl. Add the prawns to the marinade and mix well. Set aside for 30 minutes. Remove the prawns with a slotted spoon, leaving all the marinade behind in the bowl.

Melt the butter in a 8–9 inch (20–23cm) frying pan over a medium flame. When the butter has melted completely, turn heat to medium-high and immediately pour in the marinade. Stir and fry for a few minutes or until the butter separates and you have a thick bubbly sauce clinging to the bottom of the pan. Add the prawns and fold them in. Cook for a few minutes, stirring gently. Do not overcook the prawns.

Stick toothpicks in the prawns and serve immediately.

Quick-fried prawns

Tali hui jhinga

You may stick toothpicks in these prawns and pass them around with drinks or serve them as a main course.

Serves 4–6:

3 oz (75g) rice flour (use cornflour as a substitute)

2 teaspoons ground turmeric

1 tablespoon cayenne pepper

2 tablespoons ground cumin seeds

2½ teaspoons salt

About 1 teaspoon ground black pepper

Vegetable oil for deep-frying

¾ lb (350g) peeled, good quality prawns, defrosted and patted dry

A lemon, cut in half

Mix together the flour, turmeric, cayenne, cumin, salt, and black pepper.

Set about 1½ inches (4cm) of oil to heat in a deep frying pan or other utensil for deep-frying over a medium flame. Meanwhile, dip the prawns in the flour mixture and coat them thoroughly. When the oil is hot, put in as many prawns as the utensil will hold in a single layer. Fry until the prawns turn slightly crisp on the outside – just a minute or so – turning them around whenever you need to. Remove with a slotted spoon and drain on kitchen paper. Do as many batches of prawns as you need to and serve them hot, with a little lemon juice squeezed over them.

N.B. This is quite a 'fiery' dish. If you don't like your food too 'hot', you should substantially reduce the amount of cayenne pepper!

Deep-fried, stuffed, savoury pastry

Samosa

Samosas, generally eaten as a snack in India, make excellent appetizers. You may stuff them with almost anything, although traditional stuffings are either made out of spicy potatoes or ground meat. If you wish to use the ground meat stuffing, just use the recipe for minced lamb with mint (page 43). Boil away the liquid and drain the fat. Stuff each *samosa* with about 2½ tablespoons of the cooked mince. *Samosas* may be eaten with 'Fresh coriander chutney' (page 166) which serves as a dip.

Here is my recipe for *samosas* with the potato stuffing:

Makes 16

For the pastry

½ lb (225g) plain flour

½ teaspoon salt

4 tablespoons vegetable oil plus a bit more

4 tablespoons water

For the stuffing

1 lb 10 oz (725g) potatoes, boiled in their jackets and allowed to cool

4 tablespoons vegetable oil

1 medium-sized onion, peeled and finely chopped

6 oz (175g) shelled peas, fresh or frozen (if frozen, defrost them first)

1 tablespoon finely grated peeled fresh ginger

1 fresh hot green chilli, finely chopped

3 tablespoons very finely chopped fresh green coriander

3 tablespoons water

1½ teaspoons salt – or to taste

1 teaspoon ground coriander seeds

1 teaspoon garam masala (see page 18)

1 teaspoon ground roasted cumin seeds (see page 17)

¼ teaspoon cayenne pepper

2 tablespoons lemon juice

Vegetable oil for deep-frying

Sift the flour and salt into a bowl. Add the 4 tablespoons of vegetable oil and rub it in with your fingers until the mixture resembles coarse breadcrumbs. Slowly add about 4 tablespoons water – or a tiny bit more – and gather the dough into a stiff ball.

Empty the ball out on to a clean work surface. Knead the dough for about 10 minutes or until it is smooth. Make a ball. Rub the ball with about ¼ teaspoon oil and slip it into a polythene bag. Set it aside for 30 minutes or longer.

Make the stuffing. Peel the potatoes and cut them into ¼ inch dice. Heat 4 tablespoons oil in a large frying pan over a medium flame. When hot, put in the onions. Stir and fry them until they begin to turn brown at the edges. Add the peas, ginger, green chilli, fresh coriander, and 3 tablespoons water. Cover, lower heat and simmer until peas are cooked. Stir every now and then and add a little more water if the frying pan seems to dry out.

Add the diced potatoes, salt, coriander, *garam masala*, roasted cumin, cayenne, and lemon juice. Stir to mix. Cook on low heat for 3–4 minutes, stirring gently as you do so. Check balance of salt and lemon juice. You may want more of both. Turn off the heat and allow the mixture to cool.

Knead the pastry dough again and divide it into 8 balls. Keep 7 covered while you work with the eighth. Roll this ball out into a 7 inch (18cm) round. Cut it into half with a sharp, pointed knife. Pick up one half and form a cone, making a ¼ inch wide (5mm), overlapping seam. Glue this seam together with a little water. Fill the cone with about 2½ tablespoons of the potato mixture. Close the top of the cone by sticking the open edges together with a little water. Again, your seam should be about ¼ inch (5mm) wide. Press the top seam down with the prongs of a fork or flute it with your fingers. Make 7 more *samosas*.

Heat about $1\frac{1}{2}$–2 inches (4–5cm) of oil for deep-frying over a medium-low flame. You may use a small, deep, frying pan for this or an Indian *karhai*. When the oil is medium hot, put in as many *samosas* as the pan will hold in a single layer. Fry slowly, turning the samosas frequently until they are golden brown and crisp. Drain on kitchen paper and serve hot, warm, or at room temperature.

Spicy matchstick potato crisps

Aloo ka tala hua laccha

This is one of those snack foods that Indians munch noisily while watching Indian movie epics in which bandits chase weeping, but upstanding heroines and scantily clad girls shake their hips at the dashing heroes.

Serves 4–6 with drinks:

4 oz (110g) onion, peeled and coarsely chopped

2–3 cloves garlic, peeled

1 dried, hot red chilli (use more if you want the potatoes to be more than mildly hot)

1 teaspoon ground cumin seeds

$\frac{1}{2}$ teaspoon ground coriander seeds

1 lb (450g) potatoes

Enough vegetable oil to have $\frac{1}{2}$ inch (1cm) in a big frying pan

$\frac{3}{4}$–1 teaspoon salt

Put the onion, garlic, and red chilli into the container of an electric blender or food processor. Blend until you have a paste, pushing down with a rubber spatula, if necessary. Empty the paste into a bowl. Add the cumin and coriander and mix them in.

Peel the potatoes and cut them into $\frac{1}{8}$ inch (3mm) thick slices. You may use a mandolin, food processor, or knife to do this. Stack about 5 slices together at a time and cut them into $\frac{1}{8}$ inch (3mm) wide matchsticks. (You can either fry the potatoes as soon as they are cut or else leave them to soak in water and pat them dry.)

Line one very large or two smaller platters with kitchen paper and set near the stove.

Heat about $\frac{1}{2}$ inch (1cm) of oil in a deep, 10–12 inch (25–30cm) frying pan over a medium flame. When hot, put in as many of the cut potatoes as the pan will hold easily without overcrowding. Stir and fry until potatoes are golden and crisp. Remove the potatoes with a slotted spoon and spread them out on one area of the platter. Fry all the potatoes this way, spreading out each batch on the kitchen paper.

Take the frying pan off the fire and remove all but 4 tablespoons of the oil. Put the frying pan back on the medium flame and pour in the spice mixture from the bowl. Stir and fry it until it is brown and fairly dry. Take your time to do this, turning the heat down a bit if you think it is necessary. Now put in all the fried potatoes and the salt. Stir to mix, breaking up spice lumps as you do so. Drain again and serve.

Semolina halva

Sooji ka halva

This very light, fluffy halva may be eaten as a snack or at the end of a meal. It is very popular with children.

Serves 6:

1 pint (570ml) water

5 tablespoons vegetable oil or ghee (see page 25)

1 oz (25g) slivered, blanched almonds

11 oz (300g) fine-grained semolina

5½ oz (165g) sugar

2–3 tablespoons sultanas

¼ teaspoon finely crushed cardamom seeds (use a pestle and mortar for this)

Put 1 pint (570ml) water to boil in a saucepan. Once it comes to a rolling boil, turn the heat down to very low and let the saucepan sit on the back of the cooker.

Heat the oil or *ghee* in a large, preferably non-stick frying pan over a medium flame. When hot, put in the almonds. Stir and fry them until they turn golden. Take them out with a slotted spoon and leave them to drain on kitchen paper. Put the semolina into the same oil. Turn the heat to medium low. Now stir and sauté the semolina for 8–10 minutes or until it turns a warm, golden colour. Do not let it brown.

Add the sugar to the pan and stir it in.

Very slowly, begin to pour in the boiling water into the pan. Keep stirring as you do so. Take a good 2 minutes to do this. When all the water has been added, turn the heat to low. Stir and cook the halva for 5 minutes. Add the sultanas, almonds and crushed cardamom seeds. Stir and cook the halva for another 5 minutes.

This halva may be served hot or warm or at room temperature.

Vermicelli pudding

Seviyan ki kheer

In India, we use a very thin, delicate vermicelli known as *seviyan* to make this pudding. Since this is available only in Indian stores, I have worked out a recipe for the vermicelli that can be found in most supermarkets.

Serves 6–8:

2 oz (50g) unsalted butter

3 oz (75g) vermicelli, broken into 2 inch (5cm) lengths

2½ pints (1.5 litre) hot milk

¼ teaspoon cardamon seeds, crushed to a powder in a mortar

2 tablespoons sultanas

1 oz (25g) chopped almonds

½ oz (15g) finely chopped pistachios (use more almonds as a substitute)

4 oz (110g) sugar (or to taste)

Melt the butter in a heavy saucepan over a medium-low flame. Put in the vermicelli. Stay watchful now. Stir and fry the vermicelli until the pieces turn golden brown. This happens rather suddenly. Some pieces will be darker than others. That is to be expected. Pour in the hot milk and bring to a simmer. Now adjust the heat to medium-low or whatever temperature keeps the milk simmering vigorously without letting it boil over. Add the cardamom seeds, sultanas, and almonds.

Let the milk simmer vigorously for about 20 minutes. Stir frequently during this period. Add the sugar and cook another 5 minutes. You should now have about 2 pints (1.25 litres) of pudding or a bit less.

Pour the pudding into a bowl and allow to turn lukewarm. Stir a few times as this happens. A skin will form at the top. Just stir it in. Pour the lukewarm pudding into a single serving bowl or into several individual bowls (or ice-cream cups). Garnish with the pistachios, cover with cling film, and refrigerate. Serve cold.

Carrot halva

Gajar ka halva

Serves 4:

1 lb (450g) carrots

1¼ pints (700ml) milk

8 whole cardamom pods

5 tablespoons vegetable oil or ghee

5 tablespoons castor sugar

1–2 tablespoons sultanas

1 tablespoon shelled, unsalted pistachios, lightly crushed

10 fl oz (275ml) clotted or double cream, optional

Peel the carrots and grate them either by hand or in a food processor. Put the grated carrots, milk, and cardamom pods in a heavy-bottomed pot and bring to a boil. Turn heat to medium and cook, stirring now and then, until there is no liquid left. Adjust the heat, if you need to. This boiling down of the milk will take you at least half an hour or longer, depending upon the width of your pot.

Heat the oil in a non-stick frying pan over a medium-low flame. When hot, put in the carrot mixture. Stir and fry until the carrots no longer have a wet, milky look. They should turn a rich, reddish colour. This can take 10–15 minutes.

Add the sugar, sultanas, and pistachios. Stir and fry another 2 minutes.

This halva may be served warm or at room temperature. Serve the cream on the side, for those who want it.

Ice cream with nuts

Kulfi

As far as I can remember, we never made *kulfi* at home. This may well have been because it was served always to hundreds of people at wedding banquets. Only a professional *kulfi-wallah* could be entrusted with such a monstrous task. Orders were placed with him weeks in advance. On the day of the banquet, he arrived with assistants, usually his sons and brothers, carrying enormous earthenware vats. The vats were set up somewhere outdoors, usually at the edge of a vast lawn. Each vat contained lots of broken ice and, embedded in the ice, hundreds of tube shaped terra cotta containers filled with *kulfi*. Every now and then the *kulfi-wallah* would ease his arm into the vats and give its contents a knowing swish. We were never allowed to ask for a *kulfi* until the main meal, set up under brightly appliquéd tents, had finished.

Kulfi is not difficult to make at home as I have discovered in the years that I have been deprived of local *kulfi-wallas*. All you need is an adequate freezer. (If any of you have an ice cream machine, you may use it for *kulfi*.) *Kulfi* is not made with cream but with reduced milk. It helps to have a very heavy pot with an even distribution of heat for boiling down the milk. A heavy, non-stick pan would also do.

Serves 6:

$3\frac{1}{2}$ pints (2 litres) milk

10 whole cardamom pods

4–5 tablespoons sugar

$\frac{1}{2}$ oz (10g) chopped, blanched almonds

1 oz (25g) chopped, unsalted pistachios

Bring the milk to the boil in a heavy pot. As soon as the milk begins to rise, turn the heat down, adjusting it to allow the milk to simmer vigorously without boiling over. Add the cardamom pods. The milk has to reduce to about a third of its original amount, that is, to about $1\frac{1}{4}$ pints (700ml). Stir frequently as this happens. Whenever a film forms on top of the milk, just stir it in.

When the milk has reduced, remove the cardamom pods and discard them. Add the sugar and almonds. Stir and simmer gently for 2–3 minutes. Pour the reduced milk into a bowl and let it cool completely. Add half of the pistachios and stir them in. Cover the bowl with aluminium foil and put it in the freezer. (If you have an ice cream machine, you could empty the contents of the bowl into the machine and get it going.)

Put 6 small, individual cups, empty yogurt cartons or a $1\frac{1}{2}$ pint (850ml) pudding basin into the freezer.

Every 15 minutes or so, remove the ice cream bowl from the freezer and give the ice cream a good stir in order to break up the crystals. As the ice cream begins to freeze, it will become harder and harder to stir it. When it becomes almost impossible to stir, take the containers out of the freezer. Work quickly now. Divide the ice cream between the cups or empty into the pudding basin. Sprinkle the remaining pistachios over the top. Cover the cups or basin with aluminium foil, crinkling the edges to seal them. Put into the freezer and let the ice cream harden.

Mangoes

Good mangoes are amongst the best fruit on earth. They can be found in Great Britain in two basic forms, tinned and fresh. The tinned ones come sliced, or as a purée. I rarely serve the slices as I find their texture to be pathetically mushy but I do use the purée. I often chill it thoroughly and then swirl it into a bowl filled with double the amount of whipped cream. I then sprinkle some toasted almonds or pistachios over the top. It is a very simple dessert. Very refreshing too.

Fresh mangoes are another matter. If you ever see good ones (those with a strong mango aroma), such as the *alphonso* from the Bombay region, do buy them. Remember, though, that many grocers sell mangoes that are not fully ripe – those that are hard to the touch – because they have a long shelf life. Such mangoes may be ripened at home. Just wrap them individually in newspaper and then put them in a covered basket or cardboard box. Leave this container in a warm place (such as the kitchen) until the mangoes are ripe. A ripe mango should yeild slightly when pressed.

After the mangoes have ripened, they should be chilled, peeled and sliced. Mangoes do have stones. So you have to slice around them. Do not throw the stones away before nibbling off all the flesh first!

Spiced tea

Masala chai

This tea, flavoured with cinnamon, cardamom, and cloves, may be served at tea time or at the end of a meal. I love it on cold, blustery days, with some 'Spicy matchstick potato crisps' (page 190) to nibble on the side.

Serves 2:

1 pint (570ml) water

A 1 inch (2.5cm) stick of cinnamon

8 cardamom pods

8 whole cloves

6 fl oz (175ml) milk

6 teaspoons sugar (or to taste)

3 teaspoons any unperfumed, loose black tea

Put 1 pint (570ml) of water in a saucepan. Add the cinnamon, cardamom, and cloves and bring to a boil. Cover, turn heat to low and simmer for 10 minutes. Add the milk and sugar and bring to a simmer again. Throw in the tea leaves, cover, and turn off the heat. After 2 minutes, strain the tea into two cups and serve immediately.

INDEX